AN EPITAPH FOR
VOCATIONAL GUIDANCE

AN EPITAPH

FOR VOCATIONAL GUIDANCE

Myths, Actualities, Implications

RUTH BARRY and BEVERLY WOLF

Bureau of Publications

Teachers College, Columbia University

New York, 1962

PRINTED IN THE UNITED STATES OF AMERICA

PREFACE

An Epitaph for Vocational Guidance began as a textbook for the graduate course usually entitled "Occupational Information" or "Occupational Analysis" or something similar. Like most textbooks, it received its stimulus from total dissatisfaction with current texts, and its purpose was to have been to present in a theoretically sound and consistent manner the many disparate materials ordinarily comprising such a course. Then difficulties arose. We found that assumptions, specious facts, and myths could not honestly be combined into a logical whole. Eventually one question began to trouble us more and more frequently, How can one write a textbook for a course that should not be taught?

At this point, the book took on a new shape, focus, and purpose. Drawing upon our own extensive historical research into the development of the guidance movement, the unanswerable questions raised time and again by our graduate students, and the comments of our own and their counselees, we decided to analyze the theories and practices of vocational guidance. Our conclusions led us to write about the myths, the actualities, and the implications of current vocational guidance, synthesizing them into an epitaph for a field that contributed much to the development of guidance, but whose worth lay primarily in the movement it helped to foster. The purpose of the book is simply to present that analysis and our conclusions in the hope that it will allow educators, counselors, and lay people the opportunity to review their current guidance practices and to separate the wheat from the chaff.

Perhaps in one sense *Epitaph* is still a textbook for some of the traditional vocational guidance courses. Only by analysis, criticism, dissatisfaction, and the development of new constructive measures can progress be made. If this book can stimulate counselors to question and seek new theories and methodologies, its purpose will be fulfilled.

We should like to express our thanks to the secretarial assistants without whose help we could not have completed this manuscript: Mary Sall Graham of New York City; Arlene Ecklund of Vermillion, South Dakota; and Eunice Ahlberg Sliver of Worthington, Minnesota. Our deepest gratitude naturally goes to those students of all ages who have always taught us far more than we have ever taught them.

R. B.
B. W.

CONTENTS

Part II: ACTUALITIES

Part III: IMPLICATIONS

Part I

MYTHS

MYTHS ARE an integral part of every civilization. They are the collective beliefs people formulate to explain the unknown. If the beliefs represent and coincide with the wishes, hopes, and desires of the people, they become widely accepted. In proportion to their importance to the people most intimately concerned, myths achieve a sacrosanct quality that casts in the role of a heretic anyone who questions their validity. Believers rise to defend their myths because destruction of them usually heralds the abolition of the old and the rise of the new.

In this scientific age, one is tempted to think of myths as existing only in ancient civilizations or in primitive societies where people need them for explanations of the world that their science cannot substantiate. The view of the earth as the center of the universe became a myth when Copernicus showed the Ptolemaic system to be false. Beliefs become myths only after knowledge discredits them. While people hold a belief, it is an actuality. Hence myths must necessarily be relegated to the past.

Today outmoded beliefs are more generally called stereotypes or old wives' tales, modern euphemisms for myths. Many unacknowledged myths are prevalent. Some exist despite available evidence that would remove them from the realm of belief and place them properly into their mythological category. The field of vocational guidance and occupational information contains many such beliefs that should accurately be classed as myths. These are the subject of the first part of this book.

The major myths of vocational guidance furnish the foundation for current practice and methods. In essence, basic beliefs in the validity of traditional theory, the absolute quality of measurement, the applicability of occupational classification systems, the authentic factual nature of occupational information, and the actuality of realism comprise the myths.

All the myths share several characteristics. They are easily understood and increase in popular credence as school guidance programs grow in number. They seem to promise quick, simple routes to great accomplishment for individuals and society. They are speciously logical in that if one accepts the hypotheses on which they rest, the conclusions necessarily follow. Furthermore, these myths represent what everyone would like to believe possible, and herein lies their strength.

Tradition in and of itself exerts a strong influence. What has been believed and done must somehow be totally right. Analysis can occasionally shake tradition, but it alone cannot evoke change. Change and development can come about only if the followers of a tradition freely relinquish their vested interests and recognize that the originators of the beliefs were trying to explain some phenomena, explore some problems, and set up means for amelioration against the background of their own knowledge, culture, and time. Myths can be destroyed only if people keep in mind the fact that the current traditions were once innovations, battles against other then-popular myths. The originators may have believed in the precept of Junius, "I do not give you to posterity as a pattern to imitate, but as an example to deter."

Chapter 1

SINGLE THEORY

VOCATIONAL GUIDANCE suffers from an absence of discussions of possible theoretical constructs. All textbooks on vocational guidance and occupational information contain similar theoretical statements, as though there were only one basic theory. This focus upon a single theory forces its acceptance, for it offers no alternatives and no starting point for constructive criticism.

The repetition of the same theoretical position creates the myth that a single, universally accepted theory exists and the corollary myth that vocational guidance practices have a sound theoretical basis. It is true that vocational guidance began with a theory and, therefore, differs from other aspects of guidance in its possession of definite, official statements of theory and policy. It is not true, however, that these statements are unquestioned or that only a single theory exists. The only way to examine the myth of a single theory is to look at the various theories and see how they relate to one another.

The Various Theories

Theoretical concepts in vocational guidance are many and varied. Basically they can be divided into four major groups. The first of these, methodological theory, is the simplest and most familiar; it is traditional single theory. The second group, pattern theory, contains the modern attempts to establish generalizations and patterns that increase knowledge about occupations and the people in them. The third group, motivational theory, deals primarily with the reasons why people work and what satisfaction means. The fourth group, individual theory, consists of the concepts of individual occupational choice.

Vocational guidance theories present an interesting phenomenon. Methodological theory dates back to the beginnings of vocational guidance. Pattern, motivational, and individual theories date back only to the early 1950's. Being new and many, they are in the beginning stages of development and not yet related to practice. Yet someday they may combine to offer new perspectives and tools to the modern counselor.

METHODOLOGICAL. The most traditional and familiar theory deals primarily with methods of vocational guidance. From the point of view of the practitioner, only the methodological approach relates directly to the techniques he employs.

The single theory underlying all vocational guidance *practice* was formulated between 1905 and 1908 by Frank Parsons, a Boston educator and social worker interested in the problems of immigrants. His work at the Civic Service House and at Breadwinners' College, which he founded with Ralph Albertson, caused him to propose a plan for "vocational guidance" in the Boston schools. Parsons died on September 26, 1908, before vocational guidance was tried in 1909–1910, but his theory, publicized by his assistants, became the immediate *sine qua non* of all vocational guidance. Almost immediately Harvard University started a training course for counselors (1911) and enthusiastic supporters formed an association (the National Vocational Guidance Association) unofficially on November 15 and 16, 1910, and officially on October 21–24, 1913. The idea of vocational guidance spread like proverbial wildfire.[1]

These events occurred so swiftly that the myth of theory

---

[1] Every counseling student should peruse at least some of the early materials. Only thus can he make his own interpretations uninfluenced by the biases of others—even the present writers'.

grew before any evaluation could take place. Frank Parsons died before he could watch the school tryout of his theory and its results. Originally, he had based his plan for vocational guidance on only three and one-half months of work with fewer than a hundred immigrants of all ages who had sought help at his social agency. The training for vocational counselors started before anyone could be sure what these counselors should do or what their training should be. The counselors were created simultaneously with their programs. Then the theory, programs, and training were reproduced endlessly throughout the country.

The influence of Parsons' theoretical statements can be seen clearly throughout the development of vocational guidance, but perhaps the most dramatic example is a simple comparison. Parsons maintained in 1908 that the wise choice of a vocation involves "three broad factors":

. . . (1) a clear understanding of yourself, your aptitudes, abilities, interests, ambitions, resources, limitations, and their causes; (2) a knowledge of the requirements and conditions of success, advantages and disadvantages, compensations, opportunities, and prospects in different lines of work; (3) true reasoning on the relations of these two groups of facts.[2]

Exactly fifty years later, in *Occupational Information*, Baer and Roeber wrote:

Many educators of counselors follow the practice of outlining three steps in career planning: first, the study of the counselee (or self-study); second, the study of occupations; and third, the relating of the two areas of understanding.[3]

[2] Frank Parsons, *Choosing a Vocation* (Boston, Houghton Mifflin), p. 5.
[3] Max F. Baer and Edward C. Roeber, *Occupational Information* (Chicago, Science Research Associates, 2nd ed., 1958), pp. 1–2. There are many available comparisons supplied not only by experts in occupational and vocational guidance but also by general committees and the public. For example, the pamphlet *Manpower and Education* of the Educational Policies Commission of the National Education Association (1956, p. 84) starts a discussion of guidance with the confirmation of

The authors object to the implied time sequence of the statement and point out that both the study of the counselee and the study of occupations "should be pursued simultaneously as a single process."

Age in itself does not invalidate a theory if there are no new developments running counter to it or if the theory is continuously subjected to study, testing, and experimentation. Neither new developments nor evaluation affected traditional methodological theory.

Rather as standardized tests became more popular and probed hitherto unplumbed areas and as occupational information expanded quantitatively, the short cut to vocational guidance became a simple matching of the person and the job. Even today there are many large companies that for a fee subject an individual to three days of testing and recommend an occupational choice for him in terms of specific jobs. This simple approach has become exceedingly popular. It is even used by school counselors and by employment services.

The guidance practices that Parsons recommended are important because, apart from phrenology which Parsons thought might be useful, the nature of these practices has not changed. Parsons believed that lack of knowledge of job requirements and opportunities in a large city prevented immigrants from relating to the strange city environment their skills and talents developed abroad. He then realized that some of the American youngsters at his social agency had little more knowledge, a lack causing them to flounder from job to job, picking up what work they could. Hence Parsons proposed in his theory two outlines of essential knowledge. The prospective worker should know his "aptitudes, abilities, interests, ambitions, resources, limitations," and himself—the first outline of essential "facts." The worker should also know "the requirements and conditions of

---

a 1952 statement that guidance is "the high art of helping boys and girls to plan their own actions wisely, in the full light of all the facts that can be mustered about themselves and about the world in which they will work and live."

success, advantages and disadvantages, compensations, opportunities, and prospects in different lines of work"—the second outline of essential "facts." The modern school testing program and the occupational brochure are direct outgrowths of these two outlines of essential "facts."

Such was the influence of Parsons' outlines that in 1918 the Commission on the Reorganization of Secondary Education endorsed a program consisting of

1. Survey of the world's work.
2. Studying and testing pupils' possibilities.
3. Guidance in choice and rechoice of vocation.
4. Guidance in entering upon work; that is, "placement."
5. Guidance in employment; that is, "employment supervision."
6. Progressive modification of school practices.
7. Progressive modification of economic conditions.[4]

Points 6 and 7 have been ignored, but the rest of the program has continued unchanged to the present day. A glance at any vocational guidance textbook or at the recommendations for guidance set forth by major committees and school experts [5]

---

[4] *Vocational Guidance in Secondary Education,* A Report of the Commission on the Reorganization of Secondary Education (Department of the Interior, Bureau of Education, Bulletin No. 19, 1918), p. 16. Incidentally, the familiar definition appears here also on p. 10: "Vocational guidance, properly conceived, organizes school work so that the pupil may be helped to discover his own capacities, aptitudes and interests, may learn about the character and conditions of occupational life, and may himself arrive at an intelligent vocational decision." Obviously, the pupil's "ambitions, resources, limitations, and self-understanding" had fallen by the wayside and the "intelligent" decision received emphasis. (See also *Cardinal Principles of Secondary Education,* Bulletin No. 35, 1918.)

[5] Compare, for example, with the guidance programs outlined by James B. Conant, *The American High School Today* (New York, McGraw-Hill, 1959) and even his less traditional suggestions in *Education in the Junior High School Years* (Princeton, Educational Testing Service, 1960); or with those outlined by the National Manpower Council in *A Policy for Skilled Manpower* (New York, Columbia University Press, 1954).

will attest to the program's longevity. Most school counselors need look no farther than their own guidance programs for the evidence.

Again age alone is not the important point. Both theory and practice can withstand the test of age if outside changes and developments are acknowledged and if modifications take place. The outside changes have been many; the modifications, nil.

At the time he formulated his theory, Parsons had only a few psychological theories on which to draw. The writings of G. Stanley Hall and William James were available, but there is no evidence that Parsons had read the works of either man. The prevailing psychology of 1908 was faculty psychology with slight recognition given to theories of individual differences and traits. There is no evidence that Parsons had read the early writings of Sigmund Freud and Freud did not lecture in this country until after Parsons' death. Almost all important psychological theories, experiments, and developments came after 1910. Developmental, educational, and experimental psychology; dynamic, behavioristic, environmental, and other theories of personality—all developed later in the twentieth century and have had little or no influence on the methodological theory of vocational guidance.

Psychologists also developed learning theory after vocational guidance theory had gelled. Important anthropological and sociological investigations of social class, status, and structure did not appear until the latter half of the 1920's. Increasingly, these new learnings combined with psychological contributions to stress the importance of motivations, class origins, culture, values, and the wholeness of human personality. And yet, vocational guidance theory and practice continued to advocate an occupational choice based on "reasoning" about the relations of (in Parsons' words) "two groups of facts."

Still another outside development has left methodological theory fundamentally untouched. All formulations of *counsel-*

ing theory and all investigations into *counseling techniques* came after 1910. Vocational guidance methodology was and is predicated upon the outmoded assumption that information teaches, that advice and information-giving are functions of the counselor, and that vocational guidance can exist apart from "personal" guidance. After long battles with the misnamed "nondirective" counselors and clinicians, vocational experts began in the 1950's to recommend that vocational counselors allow the counselee to talk about himself a little *before* the reasoning process starts.[6] In practice, however, even this nod toward modern counseling is "more honored in the breach than the observance."

The most surprising omission from methodological theory is the failure to recognize new approaches within the area of vocational guidance itself. Pattern, motivational, and individual theory have all advanced dramatically in the past decade. Their influence has been negligible. Methodological theory still dictates practice and continues as the greatest myth in vocational guidance.

PATTERN. Whereas methodological theory is simple and direct, pattern theories are confusing and complicated, often even contradictory. Pattern theories are similar in that they supply generalizations about people and their work. They are dissimilar in focus and starting point and, therefore, in the types of generalizations that result.

Fundamentally, pattern theories are the preliminary steps to new views of the occupational choices people make and the sequences of these choices. Because they are steppingstones, they are not self-contained. That is, a theorist such as Donald Super may offer a pattern theory as a hypothesis and then, on the basis of some of the generalizations in this hypothesis, at-

[6] Cf. Robert Hoppock, *Occupational Information* (New York, McGraw-Hill, 1957), pp. 99–103, 108–11; Gertrude Forrester, *Methods of Vocational Guidance* (Boston, D. C. Heath, 1951), pp. 347–58.

tempt to formulate further generalizations about individual development and choices. Thus out of pattern theories often come individual theories.

The various pattern theories are extremely important because they furnish the basis for the eventual destruction of antiquated methodological theory and practices. The types, potential effects, and importance of each can be seen by grouping them as theories of life-stage, career, and productivity patterns.

The best-known pattern theories are those dealing with *life stages*. Essentially this group of theories attempts to apply developmental psychology and sociology to work patterns. The groundwork for the modern theories was explored in the early 1930's in Austria and Germany by Charlotte Buehler and Paul Lazarsfeld.[7] Lazarsfeld raised important issues about choices and supplied research methods and focus for later pattern investigations, but Buehler's influence was more direct. Her report contains the prototype of later American theories.

Buehler studied biographical data of people both living and dead and interviewed residents in a home for the aged in Austria. From her data, she concluded that most people go through corresponding developmental stages at similar chronological ages. Buehler labeled these life stages Growth, Exploration, Establishment, Maintenance, and Decline. She theorized that a person's vocational development as well as other aspects of his life fits into this same pattern.

American writers on occupations paid little attention to Buehler's work until 1951.[8] For anyone interested in causes and effects, the period of the late 1940's and early 1950's would make an interesting study. This period saw the publication of

---

[7] Charlotte Buehler, *Der Menschliche Lebenslauf als Psychologisches Problem* (Leipzig, Hirzel, 1933) and *From Birth to Maturity* (London, Kegan & Paul, 1935); Paul Lazarsfeld, *Jugend und Beruf* (Jena, G. Fischer, 1931).

[8] The exception was Donald Super. Pattern theory interested him early. He discussed it in articles and books, including his widely used *The Dynamics of Vocational Adjustment* (New York, Harper, 1942), but was unable to influence his vocational guidance colleagues.

Robert Havighurst's speculations about developmental tasks (1948) and the elaboration of those tasks for children and adolescents in 1950.[9] At this same time, developmental concepts began to infiltrate vocational guidance.

Two different theories of vocational life stages were offered in 1951, one by a cross-disciplinary research team made up of Eli Ginzberg, Sol W. Ginsburg, Sidney Axelrad, and John L. Herma; the other by two industrial sociologists, Delbert C. Miller and William H. Form. The Ginzberg study had more disruptive effects.

Ginzberg and his associates interviewed selected groups of boys in New York City [10] to see whether any generalizations could be established about the types of occupational choices young people make before and during college. The researchers concluded that there are three major periods through which most youngsters pass—periods of fantasy, tentative, and realistic occupational choices. The study also pointed out the great variety and number of factors that influence the young person's job choices, the shifting nature of those choices, and the interrelationship of an individual's vocational decisions and his personality development. Hence the study emphasized a concept of occupational choices, not just one, and undermined the idea that a vocational decision is a single reasoned process.

[9] Robert Havighurst, *Developmental Tasks and Education* (Chicago, University of Chicago Press, 1948); *Fostering Mental Health in Our Schools* (Washington, ASCD 1950 Yearbook, 1950). These books are still popular in teacher-training programs.

[10] See *Occupational Choice, An Approach to a General Theory* (New York, Columbia University Press, 1951). The groups were, as the authors point out, "definitely privileged." They consisted of white Anglo-Saxon males, either Protestant or Catholic, with IQ's of about 120 or above, from upper-middle class families with both parents living and together, of an age range from eleven to twenty-four, with a preference for "scientific or engineering subjects" or humanities and the social sciences. All were students at Horace Mann–Lincoln School or Columbia University. With a "control" group, the research included 91 persons. The study and its findings have received much criticism because of the severe limitations of the sample. The issues it raises, however, are worthy of further research.

Fortunately or unfortunately, the researchers incidentally charged that vocational guidance counselors have at best only a hazy theory of occupational choice: ". . . counselors have not developed a specific and explicit theory of their own. . . ." Ginzberg and his associates then deplored vocational counselors' reliance on measurement tools to the exclusion of "appropriate procedures for studying values and goals." Although the authors delineated "good reasons to explain why vocational guidance counselors have failed to explore how occupational choices are made," statements concerning the "absence of a theory of occupational choice" antagonized vocational experts.[11]

The criticism attracted irate attention and produced a variety of reactions. Many vocational guidance experts interpreted it to mean that they were working without any theory, and they hastened to reiterate defensively and vehemently the methodological theory they had clung to so long. Other experts began to rephrase methodological theory, attempting to modernize it. A few experts, although disagreeing with the actual patterns presented, agreed with the criticism and began to concentrate on new approaches to theories of individual choice. Hence the criticism more than the research per se fomented a resurgence of methodological theory in Parsons' terms, a spate of justifications of practices with slight variations in Parsons' theory, and a few new investigations.

In 1951, Miller and Form presented their theory of "work periods," similar to life stages. Because they made no damaging statements about vocational guidance theory, their study did not receive the attention accorded the Ginzberg report. Yet theirs is one of the first attempts to view occupational development as a life-long process. They established a framework of life stages expressed in terms of work and called them Preparatory, Initial, Transition, Trial, Stable, and Retired.[12] The similarity to Buehler's earlier classifications is readily apparent.

---

[11] *Ibid.*, Chapters I and III, *passim.*

[12] The complete theory is presented in Miller and Form's excellent book *Industrial Sociology* (New York, Harper, 1951), pp. 517–786.

In setting up the hypotheses which his current research will test, Donald Super presented the most complete delineation of "vocational life stages." He synthesized the generalizations of Buehler, of Ginzberg and his associates, and of Miller and Form into the following outline:

1. *Growth* (birth to age 14) with its subdivisions of Fantasy (4–10), Interest (11–12), and Capacity (13–14) indicating the major occupational choice determinants at each given age.
2. *Exploration* (15–24) including Tentative (15–17), Transition (18–21) as the youth transfers his untried decisions to the realities of employment and/or training, and Trial (22–24) as he tests his choice in actual work.
3. *Establishment* (25–44) comprised of a trial period (25–30) in which the person continues to try out his choice or to narrow it, eventually reaching no definite choice or entering the period of Stabilization (31–44), which Super claims is "for most persons . . . the creative years."
4. *Maintenance* (45–64) consisting of "continuation along established lines."
5. *Decline* (65 on) made up of a period of Deceleration (65–70) followed by Retirement (71 on).[13]

Super does not maintain that the ages assigned to the stages are fixed, for he recognizes possible variations and is seeking to test them. What is important is that he is trying to furnish a research basis for two major concepts: (1) that vocational development is "an ongoing, continuous, generally irreversible process" and (2) that it is "an orderly, patterned process."

At present, theorists trying to establish generalizations about life stages are confronted not only by such usual difficulties as sampling and interview limitations but also by others native to their genre of research. In order to study with any degree of validity the vocational development of any group of people, an investigator must select a group and wait for them to develop, a procedure lasting fifty years or so. He must also try to elimi-

[13] Condensation from *Vocational Development, A Framework for Research* (New York, Bureau of Publications, Teachers College, Columbia University, Career Pattern Study Monograph One, 1957), pp. 36–45.

nate the effects of the cultural changes that might distort his generalizations. As a consequence, theories dealing with vocational life stages are difficult, if not impossible, to prove.

The importance of these theories lies in the implications they have for further theoretical formulations. Life-stage pattern theories demand that the vocational counselor take a view of an individual's occupational development as a continuing series of choices made throughout a lifetime: (1) reaching a period of stabilization only in middle-life; (2) becoming specific when outside forces and cultural factors act as pressures; and (3) resulting from a combination of all that the individual has experienced at any given point in his development. All of these concepts run counter to methodological theory.

There are no major conflicts among the life-stage pattern theories. Confusion and contradiction enter when one turns to *career pattern* theories. Much of the confusion occurs because the major career pattern theorists are also the major life-stage pattern theorists. Yet some of the speculations about career patterns seem to contradict the concepts of life stages.

One of the earliest important career pattern analyses was done by Miller and Form. Studying a group of men in an Ohio plant, the two sociologists wanted to find out "how various job sequences reflect occupational stability and security." As a starting point they defined occupational stability as three years or more in one job, and this definition has become the generally accepted technical one. Miller and Form analyzed the work histories of their group of men and distinguished six career patterns into which they could fit these various work histories. Some men, for example, seemed to follow one kind of work and achieve stability in it. Others changed jobs and work frequently, never reaching stability. The researchers identified six specific career patterns: "stable, conventional, unstable, single trial, disestablished, and multiple trial." [14]

In 1957 Super concluded that Miller and Form's six cate-

---

[14] Miller and Form, *op. cit.,* pp. 711–12.

gories could be reduced to four. That is, any man's sequence of jobs fits into one of the following classifications of career patterns: Stable, direct progress from training to a single type of work consistently followed; Conventional, typical progress through all of the life stages discussed earlier; Unstable, a period of trial, then stability, then trial again, the sequence repeated often; and Multiple-trial, a lifelong sequence of trials in which no period of stability occurs.[15] Super points out that these career patterns apply only to men. He speculates about possible career patterns for women, but cites the total absence of evidence that might remove such speculation from the realm of guesswork.

Career pattern analyses apparently contradict but actually broaden the concepts of life-stage patterns. Only those people following a conventional career pattern, progress through all the usual life stages. The small amount of evidence available would suggest that perhaps a majority of the people eventually have a conventional career pattern. There is, however, no way at present to determine what factors produce such a pattern or in what pursuits it is most likely to occur or even whether it is a "good" or "bad" or desirable pattern.

Further career pattern research may produce some intriguing results and questions. What types of patterns are most typical of what types of work? What, if any, patterns are evident in the analyses of the careers of creative people in various fields? The possibilities are many, but concepts of career patterns are still in their infancy.

A third type of pattern theory deals with *productivity patterns* of workers. Perhaps the most widely known theorist in this area is H. C. Lehman, who in 1953 published the results of his analyses of the careers of famous men of the past.[16] He was seeking to find whether any generalizations can be made about

[15] Donald Super, *The Psychology of Careers* (New York, Harper, 1957), pp. 73–74.
[16] H. C. Lehman, *Age and Achievement* (Princeton, Princeton University Press, 1953).

the ages at which men in various fields produce their greatest quantity and highest quality of work.

Lehman concluded that generally the quantitative and qualitative high points of productivity overlap and that there are certain age spans during which men in different lines of work reach these periods of greatest productivity. In literature, for example, writers of odes tend to be young, twenty-four to twenty-eight years of age; satirists, thirty to thirty-four; tragedians, thirty-four to thirty-eight; and novelists, forty to forty-four. These findings suggest that lilting lyricism is the province of the young, satire depends upon a certain amount of disillusionment but a still youthful desire for amelioration, and that tragedy and the novel demand added experience in life. These pattern studies all depend largely upon the sample chosen and the subjective evaluations of what a man's best work is. Cultural factors are influences as are longevity probabilities for various eras. The chief importance of these studies seems to be the effect they might have on the vocational counselor and the eager parent, both of whom tend to view the entry job as the occupational choice. The young teen-ager determined to become a novelist can always point out that neither counselor nor parent need expect great accomplishments for more than twenty years.[17]

Pattern theories—life stage, career, productivity—represent new generalizations about occupational development, sequences, and choices. They mark the beginning of new concepts that may furnish the first steps toward sound future theories of vocational guidance.

MOTIVATIONAL. Motivational theory came into being as investigators began to concern themselves with the intriguing

---

[17] Wayne Dennis is currently analyzing the productivity curves of nineteenth century creative people. His analysis is not yet complete and therefore not published, but his preliminary discussions indicate that the productivity ages he is finding are later and longer than Lehman's and that there is no early or sharp decline or cessation in productivity unless the person dies. The teen-ager may here find even more ammunition to ward off pressure for early accomplishment.

question, Why do men work? The usual flip answer, Because I like to eat, does not suffice. People who have no financial needs engage in a wide variety of work. The person who says blithely that, given enough money to live, he would head for a South Pacific island and vegetate, probably could not remain idle. The answer to why men work lies neither in necessity nor in boredom, although these factors influence some people.

Early methodological theorists rarely asked this important question. Rather they seemed to accept desire to work as a fact and to proceed from that premise. Perhaps only after sociologists raised questions about status and rewards from work, after psychologists posed theories of personality and began to investigate why people do what they do, and after anthropologists supplied information and theories about work and mores in various cultures, could vocational experts turn to such questions as, Why do men work? What satisfactions do they gain from it? What personal needs does it satisfy? From the search for answers to these questions came the beginnings of motivational theories.

Various sociological studies of communities produced evidence about class structure and the points of view toward work and reasons for working characteristic of each class. Gradually these findings crept into vocational literature. Their impact seemed to be felt most directly after the publication in 1949 of a study entitled *Job Horizons*, by Lloyd G. Reynolds and Joseph Shister. These men were seeking the "causes of labor mobility or immobility which reside in the worker's own judgment of the advantages to him of retaining or changing his job." They were testing the relationship between that heretofore nebulous concept, job satisfaction, and labor mobility.

In 1947 Reynolds and Shister interviewed 800 manual workers in a medium-sized New England city. Their findings surprised vocational experts. Satisfaction with work seemed to be closely related to subjective factors rather than to the objective items so often considered of primary importance. In rank order, the manual workers seemed satisfied because of:

1. *Independence* and control on the job. They disliked excessive supervision and wanted the opportunity to use their own "initiative and ingenuity" and to voice their opinions.

2. *Good relations* with fellow workers. Status, prestige, cooperation, recognition, human relations—all fell into this category.

3. *Fairness of treatment.* The workers wanted recognition for quality work and the feeling that they were getting their just rewards in terms of the occupational structure of the company.

4. *Job interest.* The opportunity to use the skills they possessed and to have variety in their work loomed large.

5. *Physical characteristics of the job.* Here the workers mentioned three factors: the nature of the work, then the conditions of the plant, and last the type of machinery.

6. *Wages.* Even here the wages per se were integrally bound up with the other subjective attitudes.

7. *Job security.*[18]

Reynolds and Shister point out that job security is related closely to general employment; that is, job security would undoubtedly rank higher on the list in times of high unemployment.

Essentially, the study highlighted the subjective factors in job satisfaction and led to greater emphasis by theorists (chiefly in sociology) upon the motivational aspects of work. As so often happens in the occupational field, the implications of this study did not produce a direct effect upon occupational information, labor practices, or further research. Research such as this might be valuable in finding out, for example, why so many teachers leave teaching. Salaries seem to be far more important in attracting workers than in holding them in the work.

Increasingly, however, people began to speculate about why men work. Lists of reasons were numerous and idiosyncratic. In 1957 Super, attempting to synthesize the lists of others, offered "three major needs for which satisfaction is sought in work." He grouped them as (1) human relations, including

[18] Condensation from Lloyd G. Reynolds and Joseph Shister, *Job Horizons, A Study of Job Satisfaction and Labor Mobility* (New York, Harper, 1949), pp. 6–34.

:ecognition as a person (independence, fair treatment, and opportunity for self-expression) and status; (2) interesting work
 activity and satisfying work situation; and (3) livelihood incorporating current earnings and security.[19] The similarity between the reasons for job satisfaction and the reasons for working is immediately apparent. Super's list corresponds to that
delineated by Reynolds and Shister.

No definite attempt to relate motivational speculation to personality dynamics and cultural anthropology appeared until
Anne Roe applied A. H. Maslow's theory of motivation to occupations. In *The Psychology of Occupations,* Roe has presented the most thorough study available on the psychological
aspects of work and workers. Her writings, if applied, might
suggest many new frontiers for vocational guidance practice.

Roe pointed out that any full-fledged theory of personality
can be used to clarify work motivation, job satisfaction, and occupational choice. She applied a particular theory in order "to
throw into focus the dynamic and the emotional aspects of the
problem." She chose Maslow's theory because it is "human-
centered," deals with the individual as an "integrated, organized whole," and offers an "arrangement of basic needs in a
hierarchy of prepotency." Roe added the warning that although
a person's behavior is "almost always motivated, it is also almost
always biologically, culturally, and situationally determined as
well." [20]

Maslow [21] listed human needs in the hierarchy of (1) physiological and (2) safety followed by the needs for (3) belongingness and love; (4) importance, respect, self-esteem, independ-

[19] Super, *The Psychology of Careers,* pp. 3–14.
[20] Anne Roe, *The Psychology of Occupations* (New York, John
Wiley, 1956), pp. 23–39.
[21] A. H. Maslow, *Motivation and Personality* (New York, Harper,
1954). Maslow's theory has grown in popularity probably because it
is a positive approach to personality, whereas other dynamic theories
seem to focus on explanations of abnormal behavior. Maslow himself
calls it "a positive theory of motivation," a "holistic-dynamic theory."
(p. 80).

ence; (5) information; (6) understanding; (7) beauty; and (8) self-actualization. Only when the lower needs in the hierarchy are satisfied can a man seek a higher need level. Until such basic needs as hunger and thirst, shelter and a degree of safety have been met, man cannot realize the social needs expressed as those of belongingness and love. The hungry man will seek food directly or, in m ern society, take any kind of work that will give him the m. ey to buy food. The job assumes other aspects of importance only after the primary one has been satisfied.

According to Maslow, there is no hard and fast order to the last four needs. He suggests that relatively little is known about the higher needs and their ordering. Some needs are stronger in some people than in others. His list only suggests the usual order of prepotency.

Maslow's theory and its application by Roe offer a dynamic approach to motivation and job satisfaction: a person's motivations and job choices are continuous and changing. Status and recognition may be potent factors in an occupational choice for the man whose lower needs have been satisfied. If his needs for status and recognition are sated by this job, he may then seek other satisfactions in a new occupation or he may become over-sated, bored, by remaining in the same one. According to this view, man is a continually striving animal reaching toward self-actualization and fulfillment, "to become everything that he is capable of becoming." Maslow maintains that "What a man *can* be, he *must* be." Only in this way, can he "be ultimately at peace with himself," satisfied, and happy.[22] Hence motivation can vary according to the individual, his level of need, and the gratifications he seeks at any given point.

Roe states that there are practically no studies which have "noted the possible implications of Maslow's theory for occupational psychology." She cites only a study by Centers [23] as hav-

[22] *Ibid.*, pp. 91–92.
[23] R. Centers, "Motivational Aspects of Occupational Stratification," *Journal of Social Psychology*, 28:187–217, 1948.

ing implications applicable to the theory. Although direct applications have not been made, Roe concludes that in general, "In other studies, particularly of morale and of job satisfaction, there is much to support Maslow's views and nothing to contradict them. . . ." [24]

Roe's potential influence on vocational guidance practice is, unfortunately, limited by the materials she presented in her book. She related the theory specifically to occupational classifications rather than to occupational choices. As a clinical psychologist she was attempting to lay a psychological foundation for a classification system that she needed in her research on personality and occupations. The concern of vocational experts with occupational classifications has led to their concentration upon the second half of Roe's work and an almost total ignoring of the earlier parts which would most directly affect current vocational counseling concepts and practice.

The occupational motivational theory suggested by Roe could and should mark a starting point for dynamic aproaches to vocational guidance. The mere concept of changing needs negates static lists of motivations such as those frequently offered to explain why men work and why and how they seek gratifications. A dynamic approach could lay a new foundation for vocational counseling and open new avenues of study. It could do all these things and many more, but it probably will not.

The application of dynamic motivational theory virtually demands a new orientation for most vocational counselors. Can informational activities have meaning for youngsters or adults whose needs for mere existence or social acceptance overshadow every other aspect of life? Can, in fact, the present content of occupational brochures dealing primarily with the quantitative and economic aspects of work touch upon the gratifications that people really seek from a job? Can the static measures of interests, aptitudes, and abilities at any given point really be projected meaningfully if the individual's motivations and needs

[24] Roe, *op. cit.,* p. 39.

are continually changing? Can vocational counseling be a separate entity if man is viewed holistically? Can the individual himself be viewed as less than a totality? Motivational theory highlights the premise that each individual can learn, develop, and make decisions only in terms of his own dominant needs and his own values, environment, and culture at some given point. Motivational theory suggests that vocational guidance practice concentrating upon getting and giving information is peripheral, superficial, and meaningless.

INDIVIDUAL. A special category of individual theory is necessary because of the increasing popularity of "self" words. No modern guidance book can exist without extensive use of self-understanding, self-concept, self-realization, self-evaluation, self-study—the list keeps growing. Old practices are justified and old theories refurbished by the addition of this ubiquitous prefix. The category is somewhat artificial because it suggests that the theories are fully developed, which they are not. Perhaps, however, this new fad within guidance will lead to a thorough revision of theoretical concepts and a concentration upon the "self" of the individual that will have applications for guidance practice.

When in 1951 Ginzberg and his associates charged that vocational guidance counselors had no workable theory of occupational choice, these critics were talking about an absence of real individual theory. In one sense vocational guidance practice has always operated from an erroneous individual theory: that is, an individual's occupational choice is a single, reasoned process. In another sense there have always been many superficial theories emphasizing various determinants of individual choice ranging from a stress on accident and fate to that most venerable of theories—a man's occupational choice is the result of a "divine call." Despite the varieties of speculations about individual occupational choice, the Ginzberg criticism is almost as justifiable today as it was a decade ago.

The beginnings of individual theory reflect in minutiae developments in counseling theory. The publication of Carl Rogers' books teed off the acrimonious controversy between "directive" and "non-directive" counselors. The absurdities of the nomenclature and arguments will not be discussed here. The important feature is that the controversy stimulated vocational guidance people to give greater attention to counseling theory and techniques than they might otherwise have done. Prior to that time, counseling developments had attracted little attention. The controversy led to increased interest in the individual's self-concept, values, attitudes, development, frame of reference, and perceptions—the totality of the person. At a creeping pace, this view of the individual necessarily has begun to undermine traditional vocational guidance.

Individual theory is closely related to both pattern and motivational concepts. Hence it is not surprising that the greatest contributions to individual theory within the vocational field have come from the pattern and motivational theorists. Miller and Form's writings focus upon the individual from a sociological and developmental point of view. Roe, although her emphasis is elsewhere, discusses influences upon occupational development in terms of the individual. Perhaps the clearest statement of individual theory offered by a vocational guidance expert is that of Donald Super.

Super attempts to relate pattern theory to the individual. Through the life stages he traces individual development in terms of the growth of the self-concept of the person. His statement of theory is extremely valuable for several reasons. First, like Roe, Super raises many fundamental questions in connection with his own theoretical statements. These questions alone make his book essential reading whether or not the reader agrees with his theory.

Second, Super's view of occupational development as an integral part of the self-concept serves clearly to relate counseling advances to vocational guidance. His focus on self-concept raises again and again the fundamental question of whether vocational choice can justifiably be viewed as a separate entity. It challenges the very existence of the vocational counselor as a person divorced from other aspects of counseling.

Third, Super offers the first definition of vocational guidance differing from that propounded in methodological theory. With only slight modifications, vocational counselors have clung to Albert Fletcher's definition proposed at the founding of the National Vocational Guidance Association in 1913: "Vocational guidance is the selection of, the preparation for, and the placement in a life work." [25] Super's definition proposes a new concentration and a new role for the counselor: "Vocational guidance is the process of helping a person to develop and accept an integrated and adequate picture of himself and of his role in the world of work, to test this concept against reality, and to convert it into a reality, with satisfaction to himself and benefit to society." He points out that "In choosing an occupation one is, in effect, choosing a means of implementing a self-concept." [26]

Agreement or disagreement with the new definition is unimportant; its newness and its difference are its important characteristics. It marks the first definite departure from traditional sterile methodological concepts. Unfortunately Super's questions and definition have not stimulated any discussions. The apathy that has so long sustained methodological theory continues.

Summary

Pattern, motivational, and individual theories supply the potential for new theories within vocational guidance. These stirrings, however, seem thus far not to have affected vocational guidance practice, which continues to operate from the base of a myth, the single methodological theory. Perhaps the possi-

[25] *Vocational Guidance,* Papers Presented at the Organization Meeting of the Vocational Guidance Association, Grand Rapids, Michigan, October 21–24, 1913 (United States Bureau of Education, Bulletin No. 14, 1914), p. 48.

[26] Super, *The Psychology of Careers,* pp. 196–97.

bility of new theory threatens vocational counselors with the total destruction of their life-long practices. Progress as mirrored in practice may have to await a synthesis of the new theories and a policy for vocational guidance that will furnish a substitute for indefensible practices. Until this consummation, vocational guidance has no justifiable theory. It will continue to operate on the basis of the myth that a traditional methodological theory is applicable to the modern world.

Chapter 2

MEASUREMENT

PERHAPS no myths are more generally accepted in America today than those centering around the area of measurement. They
take two forms: first, that various facets of human personality
can be accurately and definitively expressed in terms of numbers;
and second, that those numbers have implications for the individual's success in various educational and vocational enterprises. Each of these versions of the myth of measurement has
enough basis in fact to make it tenacious and enough falsehood
to make it dangerous.

Americans have always sought the single exact answer to any
problems facing them—even to those which have no answers.
In the area of human personality, they have long searched for
ways of describing and pigeonholing abilities and characteristics.
At the start of the testing movement, the test score, arrived at
by respectable statistical manipulation and expressed as a discrete number, offered a way of stating the answers to questions
about people. Over the past sixty years, the test score has
become to many people one of the most important attributes
of an individual. Without regard to its applicability, accuracy,
or original meaning, such a score—or more likely today, scores
—is used in many ways that affect the individual's life. For
example, students may be sectioned into classes on the basis of
intelligence or reading test scores; employees may be selected
for executive training on the basis of personality test ratings;

girls may be hired for clerical work on the basis of clerical aptitude test scores; teachers may be hired in the order of their rankings on an achievement test administered by a school system.

Modern psychometrists are often appalled at the misuses and misunderstandings that have developed along with the popularity of their instruments. Tests are being used for purposes that were never intended, with groups for whom they are unsuitable, and in ways that are antagonistic to the best principles of measurement. Currently many testing experts are inveighing against these abuses and warning that tests are useful tools only so long as their users recognize their limitations as well as their advantages. Unfortunately these warnings have not as yet had much effect upon the uses to which tests are put in schools, colleges, and industries. Parents, too, are becoming concerned about what they see as misuses of tests. While some parental criticism may be attributed to partisanship for their own children, many of their complaints are amply justified.

Educators have been among the chief offenders in the misuse of tests; the current ground swell against testing stems primarily from school abuses of these tools. Administrators, teachers, and counselors have all contributed to the misuse of tests in the school program, but it is with the counselors who are presumably trained in measurement that most of the blame lies. Hence any treatment of vocational guidance and occupational information requires a consideration of the kinds of tests used and their inherent weaknesses, their uses and misuses in working with students, and the reasons for abuses.

Tests and Test Scores

Almost 130,000,000 tests were given to students in 1960, according to one *New York Times* report, and the number has surely increased. Despite this proliferation in testing, only five basic types of tests are a part of the school program: intelligence or scholastic aptitude, other aptitudes, achievement, interest, and personality. The first three are the most commonly given tests, with interest inventories becoming more popular as guidance gains support, and the so-called personality tests gaining as more money is invested in testing programs. These five kinds of tests make up the bulk of the testing done in the schools and provide the basis for much of the advice and counsel offered by school personnel to students.

INTELLIGENCE TESTS. Any discussion of intelligence tests must start with the question, What is intelligence? and the answer, We do not know. Some wits contend that intelligence is whatever the intelligence tests measure, but this definition, however apt, is not helpful. Essentially there are as many definitions of intelligence as there are people devising tests of it. Sample definitions include the ability "to reason well," "to see relationships," "to adjust to new situations," "to profit by experience," "to carry on abstract thinking," or simply "to learn." All of these abilities either singly or in combination enter into most of the definitions of intelligence.

Especially important in our particular society is the ability to deal with such symbols as words and numbers. Because work with words and numbers is the particular province of the schools, intelligence tests have in recent years increasingly been called tests of scholastic aptitude. This phrase seems to be more appropriate for a title and more descriptive of what the tests actually measure. Moreover, it seems to be easier to pinpoint the meaning of scholastic aptitude than to define intelligence. The fact remains, however, that there is no general agreement on what intelligence is or how it functions.

The content of tests of intelligence shows equal variety. The tasks posed may include word meanings by synonyms or antonyms, numerical problems, spatial relationships, analogies in words or diagrams, reading comprehension, similarities, logical selection, and perception. Not all tests include all of these kinds of problems, but there is considerable similarity in the items on many of the group intelligence tests. And yet no two tests are precisely alike or attempt to measure precisely the same thing. Hence scores from these tests are not comparable. An individual may have as many different scores of intelligence as the number of different tests he takes.

Scores on intelligence tests can be reported as percentile rankings; should be reported as standard scores, which are more respectable statistically; but are most frequently reported as Intelligence Quotients (IQ's). IQ is the result of dividing mental age by chronological age and multiplying by 100. In this equation, mental age is an estimate of the level of mental activity of which a child is capable. For example, a child who can solve problems and answer questions that the average eleven-year-old can handle is said to have a mental age of 11, regardless of his chronological age. If the child is 11 years old, his IQ is 100; if the child is 10, his IQ is 110; if he is 12, his IQ is 92. The IQ as a score is the natural outgrowth of the theoretical basis for the Stanford-Binet Test of Intelligence. No other test is so constructed as to produce a result expressed as mental age from which IQ is easily calculated. All other IQ scores are derived statistically from the raw scores on the particular test in imitation of the Binet concept. The IQ score has had tremendous popularity among educators and laymen alike and, despite its many obvious disadvantages, continues in use even in the face of the disapproval of many psychometrists.

The most serious disadvantage of the IQ concept is its inapplicability to adults. Mental age is based upon the idea that mental growth resembles physical growth and occurs at a relatively stable rate during childhood and adolescence. Recent studies have contradicted the assumption that mental growth, like physical, stops in the late teens or early twenties. Apparently mental development continues throughout life in a different, less spectacular, but nevertheless significant way. In the fraction that is IQ, the denominator grows ever larger while the numerator, depending upon the test used, increases more slowly or even declines. The result is that adult IQ's decrease unless some statistical correction is made. A concept that contradicts both experience and research is not particularly workable.

Intelligence tests provide excellent illustration for a number of generalizations about all types of tests. The first of these is that *almost without exception an individual test is more accurate and descriptive of the individual than a group test.* The two common individual tests of intelligence, the Revised Stanford-Binet Test of Intelligence and the Wechsler-Bellevue Intelligence Scale, provide the examiner with a far better and more comprehensive understanding of the individual's mental functioning than any group test. Both tests require specially trained examiners and are time-consuming to administer, so they are not used in the schools except with students who present atypical problems. Despite their many advantages, even these tests share some of the weaknesses of group tests, which are the major school tools.

The second generalization stresses that *all tests investigate only a sample of the individual's behavior at a given time.* No single test can give a complete picture of intellectual functioning. The test results are closely related to the time at which it is given. A single IQ obtained ten years ago is not a satisfactory estimate of the individual's intellectual operation today. A pattern of scores obtained on different forms of the same instrument over a period of time is far more likely to produce a clearer picture of whatever is being measured. One hundred questions, no matter how searching, posed once give a totally inadequate sample of individual functioning.

The third generalization is probably the most important and the most frequently ignored. *No test score can be regarded and used as a discrete number.* A test score is an estimate, not an absolute, and incorporates within its numerical expression not only some rating of the individual but also errors of the testing instrument. Even a carefully researched test has inherent errors. It is possible to compute the standard error of measurement (or standard error of a score) for a particular group of testees, and correct scores to some extent upon the basis of this figure.[1] Standard error of measurement can then be used to establish a range within which the student's score probably falls. If the IQ is 120 and the standard error 10, then the range is 120±10 or 110 to 130. Despite this correction, the odds are only about 2 to 1 that the student's "true" score lies within the range.[2]

The concept of range of score negates many current uses of test scores within the schools—particularly the uses of IQ's. Consider the scores of four students, together with the probable ranges of those scores.

Pupil	IQ	Range
Sam	120	110–130
Mary	133	123–143
Joe	129	119–139
Pam	101	91–111

Who is the brightest of the four? Possibly Mary, but not necessarily. When one compares the ranges of the scores, even Pam cannot be excluded, because the odds are only 2 to 1 that her score lies within this range. Her score could be above or below it. Should Joe be excluded from the class for the gifted, which consists of children with IQ's 130 and above? Joe's true score may well lie above 130 or it could be below. The overlaps in the ranges of the first three students make it virtually impossible

[1] The counselor who does not have figures to compute such a correction will find the number 10 a useful approximation. For most group tests of intelligence and most groups of students, 10 is probably too low but it is an easy number to use and reminds the counselor that IQ is not absolute. Needless to say, the counselor should compute the standard error of measurement for the tests he administers.

[2] According to some statisticians, this use of the standard error of measurement is not entirely impeccable. For the counselor working with individual students, the humanitarian aspects involved in using a range of score rather than a discrete score seem to justify minor inaccuracies of that range.

to distinguish among them on the basis of IQ score alone. To repeat, a test score, particularly an IQ score, is not an absolute and cannot be used as though it were.

Closely related to the foregoing generalization is the fact that *all tests are adulterated by factors other than those they were intended to measure.* Intelligence tests, for example, attempt to measure the aptitude or potentialities of the student for the types of intellectual activity carried on in school. If the intelligence test is a group one, the student has to read the questions. Indirectly, therefore, the intelligence test result depends upon the student's achievement in reading and constitutes to some extent a measure of his reading skill. The retarded reader will score low on group IQ tests regardless of his true intellectual capacity.

Reading is probably the most important single adulterant of tests, but other factors may also contribute. Arithmetic achievement has an effect similar to that of reading because most group intelligence tests include a section devoted to numerical reasoning. If the student has had considerable practice with the arithmetical word problem, he is likely to be able to complete more problems correctly in the time allowed than is the student to whom these are less familiar.

Experience also tends to depress or elevate test scores and not always in the way expected. Suppose a boy has gone skating and fallen through the ice or seen his friend do so. If on a test he is given the word "dangerous" and asked to pick out a synonym from the three alternatives, "secure, thin, unsafe," he is likely to select "thin" rather than "unsafe," the correct answer, because thin ice is part of his experience of danger. Similarly, the bright child who is given the word "orchestra" and told to mark the one word that tells what the orchestra always has may select "violins" from the four alternatives, "violins, instruments, drums, conductor." This student may know that both orchestras and bands have instruments, but the orchestra differs through its inclusion of stringed instruments. The bright, subtle child who marks "violins" is right, but he would be scored wrong.

Quite often such children are penalized on intelligence tests for too advanced knowledge and too great subtlety.

On the other hand, standardized tests do eliminate some adulterants present in teacher-made tests. Teachers and counselors in one school were puzzled by the discrepancy between the formal test scores and the class test scores of one student. This youngster scored appreciably higher on the standardized tests. Observation and interviews led to the discovery that this student was a singularly slow writer who could show her ability when she could mark an answer sheet but not when she had to write out her answer. Hence all tests measure not only what they are presumed to measure but other abilities as well, and their results are affected by abilities other than the one or ones supposedly measured.

The fifth generalization about tests concerns the age of the test. *All tests tend to deteriorate with age.* This decline in the power of a test is not the fault of the test makers, but results from our changing world and the new developments which ruin the value of certain questions. Currently such questions as, What does espionage mean? What does sword mean? What does hari-kari mean? on the Vocabulary section of the Wechsler Intelligence Scale for Children may have lost some of their discriminatory power. The current television emphasis upon sword play and espionage has familiarized many children with the words, while the greater attention to things Japanese since World War II has made the word hari-kari almost as familiar. Three questions may not seem like many, but in a sample of forty, these three can exert considerable influence upon the final score. If a test is over twenty years old, as many group tests are, one can usually find more than three items which have lost their discriminatory power.

Test construction is a lengthy and costly process. This explains why many tests are allowed to become outmoded before they are revised. Revision of a widely researched instrument like the Stanford-Binet means that much of the research has to be redone in terms of the new version. Prediction studies and com-

parisons with other tests have to be redone in order to re-establish
these relationships for the new version of the test. Hence both
age and revision affect test scores and limit the usability of the
instrument, at least for a period of time.

The sixth generalization is particularly important for counselors. While predictions based upon the test scores of groups
of students can be made with some accuracy, *predictions on the
basis of the test scores of an individual are at best extremely
risky.* Prediction is commonly done by computing the degree of
relationship between two groups of data, for example the IQ's
of a large number of students and their college grade-point
averages. In many of the studies using these two kinds of data
the degree of relationship expressed as a correlation coefficient
proves to be about .45. The size of this coefficient implies the
existence of some relationship, but indicates that it is not too
strong. What then is the predictive value of such a relationship? According to Franzblau, ". . . coefficients below .40 do
not yield a guess even 10 per cent better than chance. To yield
a prediction which is 25 per cent better than a chance or random guess, the correlation must be at least .66." [3] Despite this
statistical fact, counselors are making predictions for individual
students about success in college on the basis of intelligence
and other tests. Guidance authors are recommending the practice of prediction when the relationships between the variables
clearly indicate that such predictions can be at most only 25
per cent better than mere guesswork.

Prediction is especially risky when it is viewed in terms of
the individual for whom it is done. The inherent errors of the
test itself, the inconclusiveness of the relationship between the
predictor and what is being predicted make it virtually impos-

[3] Abraham N. Franzblau, *A Primer of Statistics for Non-Statisticians*
(New York, Harcourt, Brace, 1958), p. 88. This is a valuable book for
the counselor who is not a statistician and yet wishes to examine critically
some of the current statistical mayhem in the guidance area. Franzblau
writes clearly and simply and answers many of the questions on statistical
interpretation that are omitted from or buried in the detail of the traditional statistics text.

sible for the counselor to predict a student's performance with any degree of surety.

One final generalization is especially important in light of the current interest in gifted students: *no test measures as accurately at the extremes as it does at the middle.* In other words, no test can distinguish between two highly gifted students as well as it can between two students whose scores are more nearly average. This statement is equally true for students whose scores are at the bottom of the scale, although in this instance counselors are less likely to attach significance to a point or two of difference in score.

The seven generalizations are not intended to scare counselors away from using tests, but rather from abusing them. Intelligence tests are the most abused of any tests administered in the schools today. Since they can be a valuable tool, the counselor needs to give careful thought to his use of them in his program and in his individual counseling with students.[4]

APTITUDE TESTS. Strictly speaking, intelligence tests could be included under this heading, but their importance in school testing programs warrants devoting a separate section to them. Aptitude tests are an attempt to measure an individual's potentialities for future development along certain lines. They seek to answer such questions as, Will this girl be likely to do well in the study of French? Has this boy the potential for mechanical work? Does this student have the capacity for musical studies? Does this student have the finger dexterity that may permit him to develop into a watchmaker?

Aptitude tests are of two main types, the batteries and the tests for specific potentialities. Aptitude batteries consist of a

---

[4] This section has intentionally omitted the discussion of certain concepts which may more properly be covered in a measurement course. The counselor should, of course, know about the reliability and validity of tests, be familiar with procedures for evaluating tests before he selects them for his school program, and understand the statistical procedures that he should routinely carry out on all test results. The attempt here is to present some generalizations that are not ordinarily emphasized in measurement courses.

number of tests designed to produce a picture of the individual's capabilities along various lines. The more general batteries usually include separate tests of spatial and abstract reasonings, verbal, numerical, mechanical, clerical, and language abilities. Such a battery produces results resembling those of intelligence tests, but gives some idea of the relative strengths of the various abilities that are thought to enter into what is called intelligence. Aptitude batteries do not, of course, yield IQ scores. Some are less concerned with verbal and reasoning aptitudes and concentrate more heavily on memory, coordination, patterns, precision, assembly, and judgment. Rather special tests, which may or may not be batteries, are those designed to measure aptitudes for particular vocations such as nursing, medicine, law, engineering, dentistry, teaching, and selling.

In addition to aptitude batteries, there are tests for specific potentialities along mechanical, clerical, musical, and artistic lines as well as for such physical aptitudes as finger dexterity, motor speed, vision, and hearing. These tests represent attempts to detect in individuals the potential for further development in the areas covered by the tests.

Aptitude testing is subject to all the vicissitudes that plague intelligence testing, but it is particularly subject to adulteration by achievement. The student who has had good mathematical training is likely to score high on the numerical section of an aptitude battery. The boy who has had considerable experience in taking objects apart and putting them together again may do well on a test of mechanical aptitude. This contamination faces the test constructor with a problem reminiscent of the old riddle, Which comes first, the chicken or the egg? Which does come first, the aptitude for taking things apart or the achievement represented by learning to do so, and how much of each does the test measure? Much has been made of the fact that boys score significantly better on tests of mechanical aptitude than do girls, but here the achievement factor cannot be discounted. Early in their lives boys receive mechanical toys and imitate their fathers' mechanical pursuits, while girls do not.

Mechanical aptitude tests may well be measuring a particular achievement closely related to sex roles in modern society. In many instances, it is impossible to be certain whether a test is measuring aptitude or achievement.

Because they attempt to measure potential, aptitude tests should be good predictors. That is, a test designed to measure aptitude for language study should predict with reasonable accuracy those students likely to succeed in first-year French.[5] Similarly, an aptitude test designed to measure the individual's capacity to profit from training for a vocation should be able to predict with reasonable accuracy his success in that work. Aptitude tests fail here too, for Thorndike and Hagen say, ". . . there is no convincing evidence that aptitude tests or biographical information of the type that was available to us can predict degree of success within an occupation. . . ." Recognizing all the limitations of their study, these authors continue, "We should view the long-range prediction of occupational success by aptitude tests with a good deal of skepticism and take a very restrained view as to how much can be accomplished in this direction." [6] Aptitude tests as predictors are questionable at best and do not deserve the inordinate faith placed in them by many educators and counselors.

One other point deserves mention in connection with aptitude tests and their relation to vocational planning and choice. Most of the current tests were planned, developed, and standardized in the 1930's. The tests most closely related to particular occupations were standardized against workers then in those

[5] Reasonable accuracy might be defined as 50 per cent better than chance. If it is, then the test results must have a correlation of at least .86 with grades in French. In the studies of most prognostic tests as predictors the correlation is far lower. Many aptitude tests have not been studied sufficiently to provide any correlations.

[6] Robert L. Thorndike and Elizabeth Hagen, *Ten Thousand Careers* (New York, John Wiley, 1959), p. 50. This study has created remarkably little stir in the guidance area despite the fact that Thorndike is quoted in an interview in the New York *Herald Tribune* of December 13, 1959, as saying, "There's been too much enthusiasm for aptitude testing. We don't know enough to guide a man into a specific career."

fields and, in the thirties, most of those workers were men. Only since World War II have women become an important segment of the labor force. As a consequence, aptitude tests must be carefully scrutinized to make sure that their research structure permits their use with women as well as men. Here is another instance in which the age of the test may make it inapplicable to the needs of today.

Both intelligence and aptitude tests have their faults and their pitfalls for the unwary user. These disadvantages cannot, however, be blamed on the psychometrists who have long been warning that tests are good only when they are used for the purposes for which they were designed and interpreted with suitable caution. Counselors, especially in the vocational area, need to heed this advice.

ACHIEVEMENT TESTS. Achievement tests, unlike aptitude tests, are designed to measure what a student has already learned in a particular subject-matter area or areas. They attempt to measure actual learning rather than potential for learning.

Achievement tests may be subdivided into two types, the battery and the single test. The battery usually covers vocabulary, spelling, language usage, arithmetic, reading, social studies, and science or some combination of these. The battery is used primarily in elementary and junior high schools to determine how children compare with one another in their learnings and to contrast children's learnings in one school or school system with those in another. The single test measures student learning in a particular course, such as first-year algebra or American history. It is used more frequently in high schools where differences in programming make the use of a complete battery for every student unfeasible.

Achievement tests are usually designed after careful study of course syllabi, textbooks, and other material relating to the subject and age group to be tested. A test based upon this procedure is said to have curricular validity in that it measures the learning of the materials usually presented in a particular grade or subject. Whether or not the test actually has curricular validity, however, depends upon the person using it as well as upon the one who designed it. If an administrator chooses a test that covers materials not handled by the teachers in his school, then the test has limited curricular validity for his school and the results are not comparable with those obtained from pupils in other schools. Hence the person selecting an achievement test has to be sure that the material it covers is applicable to the materials that have been taught.

Achievement tests suffer from a number of flaws. Some of these tests are designed to fit into a school period and are consequently too short to probe adequately the students' learnings; others, claiming to have national norms, may have norms that are by no means representative of the nation. These are minor flaws, however, when one considers the major difficulty in achievement testing, one over which the test makers have no control. This difficulty might be called the human circle effect. It operates as follows: a teacher gives her class an achievement battery and the scores fall below the norms. She is disappointed and the following year reshapes her teaching somewhat to bring it in line with the tests. The scores in the second administration are somewhat better so she again slants her teaching toward the test. At the end of five years the test is, to some extent, determining the curriculum instead of the curriculum determining the test. In some areas of the country where the quality of teaching is poor, this human circle effect might be highly desirable, but it is questionable whether tests should dictate curriculum in all school systems. Interestingly, the Educational Testing Service designed its Sequential Tests of Educational Progress (STEP) with this effect in mind. One purpose of these tests was to make them so hard and so searching that teachers would have to teach up to them.

Whether or not the human circle effect is desired, it usually operates. Many schools will find that using tests over a period of time leads to a gradual rise in mean and median and a decline in standard deviation. Does this represent a true rise in the achievement of the students or does it mean they are being given extra work in the areas covered by the test? Probably the latter, but it would be a very difficult point to prove. Some teachers tend to view achievement tests as a device for evaluating the quality of their teaching and this fear can exert considerable effect upon the relationship between the test and what is taught.

Despite these objections, achievement testing can be worth while from the point of view of both the administrator and the counselor. [Such testing affords the opportunity to discover those students who need remedial work or those who need extra help in one phase of the work so that they will not need extensive remedial aid later in their school careers.] Achievement tests also provide some standards for comparison among schools or school systems.]

INTEREST INVENTORIES. The so-called interest "tests" are actually inventories of a person's preferences, his likes and dislikes, at a given time. Definitions of interests, like those of intelligence, are not identical. [There is growing agreement that a person's preferences are strongly influenced by his environment and experiences, but no one knows whether or not any interests are innate.] Observation lends support to the belief that what a person does not know, he tends to say he dislikes. The youngster offered a new food, often says he "dislikes" it. Even adults agree that ripe olives, caviar, snails, and eels are "acquired tastes" involving experience, motivation, practice, learnings, and many psychological factors. Experiences and people's reactions to them vary. [Strong concludes that "The different reactions, we suspect, arise because the individuals are different to start with." [7]]

If interests or preferences depend on so many variables, what can be measured? Again no one is quite sure. Strong claims that, whatever is being measured, "Whether interests, preferences, values, goals, or what have you, [the interest inventory]

[7] E. K. Strong, Jr., *Vocational Interests of Men and Women* (Palo Alto, Stanford University Press, 1943), p. 683.

measures something very stable and permanently possessed that contributes very greatly to occupational choice." [8] Whatever this something may be, interest inventories attempt to get at it.

Essentially, interest inventories require a person to respond to definite questions in terms of likes and dislikes or to make choices among listed items. For example, a person may check whether he likes, dislikes, or is indifferent to such specific occupations as draftsman, orchestra conductor, and undertaker; school subjects; amusements; various activities; even such peculiarities of people as pessimism, Bolshevism, or irreligiousness. Some inventories ask the examinee to rank in order his choices among such groups of items as "Sell artists' supplies, Grow seed for florists, Raise white mice for scientists" or "Cook a meal, Mend a broken toy, Give someone a shampoo." Whatever the specific contents of the inventory may be, all inventories attempt to relate the examinee's responses to those believed to be important in general fields of endeavor or in specific vocations.

The two most widely used interest inventories are the Strong Vocational Interest Blank for Men [9] and the Kuder Preference Record. These two instruments are totally different and cannot be used interchangeably. In fact, no two interest inventories probe the same factors or produce results that are comparable in any sense.

The Strong VIB is one of the most extensively researched instruments in all of measurement. It is experimentally derived. Over the years, researchers have tried to identify the significant interests of people in specific occupations and thus to establish scales by which other people having these same interest patterns might also be identified. There are about 50 scales for men.[10]

[8] "Nineteen-Year Followup of Engineer Interests," *Journal of Applied Psychology*, 36:74, April 1952.
[9] There is a Strong Vocational Interest Blank for Women but it is extremely limited. Validation studies are lacking. Research on the occupational interests of women is barely underway.
[10] The number of occupational scales varies as old scales are withdrawn or revised and new scales added. In addition to the occupational scales, there are four non-vocational scales covering masculinity-femininity, ma-

The inventory itself contains 400 items, including both preference questions and forced choices as well as a self-rating of "present abilities and characteristics." The Strong VIB is a self-contained instrument; that is, it is valid only in terms of the specific occupations for which there are scales. Because it is experimentally derived, it is limited by the amount and types of materials the researchers used. Much research is necessary before a new scale can be added to it or an old one revised. Hence many of the scales are out-of-date.

The Kuder Preference Record differs greatly from the Strong. Whereas the Strong is strictly an adult inventory, the Kuder is designed for use with junior and senior high school students as well as with adults. Whereas the Strong is based upon research, the Kuder is not. The validation studies done on the test are limited and questionable.

The Kuder presents 168 sets of forced choices such as those illustrated earlier. The patterns of interests identified from these choices are related to general areas of interest designated as mechanical, computational, scientific, persuasive, artistic, literary, musical, social service, clerical, and outdoor. Because the Kuder is used with people of such varying ages, the test makers have included a short glossary to aid interpretation of the questions. The ability to read the choices meaningfully affects significantly the interest patterns that result. The Kuder Preference Record is becoming increasingly popular in schools throughout the country.

Interest inventories suffer from the general weaknesses of sampling and error of all objective tests. They can be readily and easily faked because the appropriate choices are obvious

---

turity of interest, occupational level, and studiousness. Counselors using the Strong should examine the manual carefully, especially the sections describing the original groups. Many of them are atypical of the total population and raise many questions about sampling. Sampling methods are also questionable in terms of the validation study which was done on a group of Stanford students followed through the years. There is general agreement that the Strong is better for high-level occupations than for others.

even to the most naive. The Strong manual warns that the
tests are not to be used as selection devices. Interest inventories
are perhaps more easily outdated than other instruments. The
Strong, for example, asks the examinee to choose the three men
he would most, and the three men he would least, like to be.
The list includes Luther Burbank, Enrico Caruso, Thomas Edi-
son, Henry Ford, Charles Dana Gibson, J. P. Morgan, John J.
Pershing, William H. Taft, Booth Tarkington, and John Wana-
maker. This question has probably lost whatever significance it
had in 1930. And yet it cannot be modernized because changes
would distort the research.

In addition to the general weaknesses, interest inventories
pose problems peculiarly their own. The first of these deals with
the stability of interests or whatever the interest inventories measure. Ten to twenty years ago psychometrists thought a person's
interest patterns were set by age fifteen. Today many measurement experts believe that interests do not stabilize until about
age twenty-five and that they remain stable through middle age.
Is either of these estimates right? No one knows. Do the
changes in age reflect basic changes in our culture?

Most of the information on stability of interests comes from
research done on the Strong VIB. The Strong researchers warn
that interest patterns of adolescents change so dramatically that
the inventory can be used best with people between the ages of
twenty-five and fifty-five, fairly well with people between twenty
and twenty-five, and should never be used with boys below
seventeen unless they are exceptionally mature. If one accepts
these findings about interest stability, then the use of the Kuder
in junior and senior high schools with students younger than
seventeen is at best a waste of money and time, and at worst
dangerous in narrowing interests before the youngster has had
a chance to develop them.

The second major problem of interest inventories concerns
similarities of interests. There are many more similarities than
differences among the interests of people. This fact in itself
suggests that general culture and the common types of experi-

ences and learnings people share within a culture are extremely influential. The relatively small amount of research points out that the greatest difference in interest patterns exists between those characteristic of men and those characteristic of women. In fact, the greatest variation exists between the interests of fifteen-year-old boys and those of adult women. Only a few tested differences occur among people in different occupations. Although these differences may be statistically significant they may not be great. Yet differences, not similarities, are the basis for interest inventories. No one knows whether the relatively small number of differences in interests probed on inventories are the most important ones in occupational choice. Until more is known about similarities and differences in interests per se and their relationship to a large number of occupations, interest inventories can have little meaning.

Interest inventories present a third problem, often ignored by counselors. As measured by the means now available, interests have little or no relationship to a person's intelligence, aptitudes, and general ability. This point is important because it negates the picture of a person the counselor often tries to create out of a series of tests. A person interested in science may have no aptitude for or ability along that line. The counselor cannot generalize from an interest inventory, although many times he tries to do so.

The fourth major problem concerns the purpose of interest inventories and their relationship to the school counseling program. Basically, all interest inventories are a means of narrowing a student's choices. The manual accompanying the Kuder makes this point explicit: "Even if an individual thinks of surveying the whole range of occupations, he is likely to be discouraged by the immensity of the task. He needs some way of narrowing the field so he can investigate occupations most likely to suit him." But does the junior or senior high school student need to be "narrowed"? Is not the purpose of occupational information to allow him to broaden his horizons and experiences?

Interest inventories tend to channel a student's interests and investigations along the lines suggested by the inventory. Such channeling is particularly detrimental for the gifted or creative student. Modern studies of the gifted are increasingly highlighting the point that the interest patterns of this group tend not to become specific early. The gifted student usually possesses great intellectual curiosity and is more likely than his slower counterpart to investigate an area until his curiosity is satisfied and then turn to other pursuits. Interest inventories are even less valid with the gifted and creative than with other groups and carry with them greater dangers of limiting because the gifted student tends to be the most sensitive and perceptive. The counselor must weigh the uses of interest inventories in terms of their purpose. He must consider carefully the use of the most limiting one available, the Strong. Although statistically the soundest, the Strong yields results in the narrowest possible terms—about 50 specific occupations.

The major weaknesses of interest inventories make them extremely questionable instruments for school use. If a counselor balances the dangers of using them against the possible advantages for the group with which he is working, he can come to only one conclusion: interest inventories should not be a standard part of a school testing program.

PERSONALITY TESTS. Personality tests are of two types, group and individual. Because the individual tests are time-consuming to administer and interpret, they are rarely used in the schools. Group tests of personality, however, are gradually becoming a part of many school testing programs, thanks to the current emphasis upon testing and the desire of many school administrators to have a "complete" program.

Personality tests are not really tests at all, but rather attempts to inventory an individual's feelings and attitudes about himself and other people. The following sample questions, selected at random from an assortment of personality measures, give some idea of the kinds of questions asked and the form the answers are to take. In each the subject is to select the response that best describes him:

Queer, unpleasant feelings in the body	Often At Times Seldom Never
Worry about sex matters	Often At Times Seldom Never
Do you often contribute new ideas in your work?	Yes ? No
Do you have more love for your mother than for your father?	Yes No
Do you feel inclined to tremble when you are afraid?	Yes No
Do you feel that people don't like you?	Yes No
Do you ever cross the street to avoid meeting someone?	Yes No ?
Does admiration gratify you more than achievement?	Yes No ?

There are no "right" answers to the questions posed, and scores based upon these answers cannot be viewed in terms of "good" or "bad" or "high" or "low." Presumably they tell something about the person.

A personality inventory is merely a structured interview. It is designed to elicit the kinds of information about a student that can better be discovered through talking with him. *Supposedly* these inventories save time for the counselor; actually they do not. In a study by Darley, using the Bell Adjustment Inventory to discover which of 800 students had adjustment problems, the Inventory designated correctly 40 students as having problems of home adjustment, missed 41, and mistakenly attributed such problems to 73. In the area of emotional adjustment, 32 students were correctly identified, 42 falsely identified, and 75 missed. The Inventory results were checked against

counselor interviews over the period of a year.[11] Results such
as these are of no help to the counselor, nor can such a test
save him time if he must continually check its results.

Darley's study points up a fact well known among measurement people—most personality measures are of such doubtful
validity that their use is unlikely to achieve the purposes for
which they were intended. In his summaries of the many validity studies done on these tests, Ellis finds the tests have only
slight validity in distinguishing among *groups* of adjusted and
maladjusted people and even less validity in the diagnosis of
individual adjustment.[12] For the school counselor, a test which
fails in its assessment of the individual is worthless and the
administration of such tests as a routine procedure in the schools
is a waste of time, effort, and money.

Personality tests suffer from one serious defect that contributes
to their general ineffectiveness—they are the most easily faked
of all tests. Any test, of course, can be faked to some extent.
The girl who does not want to appear to be too bright can de-
liberately answer questions incorrectly and so lower her intelligence test score. It is less easy, however, to elevate such a score.
Anyone with a modicum of psychological sophistication can
select the "well-adjusted" answers to personality inventory questions. Moreover, anyone can easily lie in response to the more
personal or value-ridden questions. None of the inventories
most generally used in the schools attempts to investigate this
lie factor and its influence on the individual score.

The defenders of group personality tests claim that good administration of them can overcome much of the falsification of
answers. But it cannot. Unfortunately the questions are such

[11] John G. Darley, "Tested Maladjustment Related to Clinically Diagnosed Maladjustment." *Journal of Applied Psychology*, 21:632–42, December 1937.

[12] Albert Ellis, "The Validity of Personality Questionnaires." *Psychological Bulletin*, 43:385–440, September 1946; also "Recent Research
with Personality Inventories." *Journal of Consulting Psychology*, 17:45–
49, 1953.

that they raise the defenses of the individual student and bring into operation all his ego-protective mechanisms. Too many of the questions are of the "Have you stopped beating your wife?" type, and students resent being forced to answer yes or no when neither is true. Even trust in and rapport with the examiner are not enough to overcome the tendency to falsify answers if the student is hostile toward the school or uncertain of the use which will be made of the results.

Perhaps the most serious defect of personality tests is that most of them are pretty haphazard from the theoretical point of view. Few of them are closely related to any theory of personality and often the orientation of the test maker has to be inferred from the words he uses to designate the different scoring keys. Most of the test manuals contain very little information about the theory, if any, underlying the particular design of the test. This lack of a sound theoretical basis makes the scores on these tests even more open to question and the interpretation of them even more problematic.

There are a few personality measures which have a sounder base or are more imaginative than those discussed above, but none of them is suitable for routine school use. The Minnesota Multiphasic Personality Inventory (MMPI) is available in two forms: an individually administered card-sort version and a group paper-and-pencil version. The card-sort form has had considerable research and is statistically more respectable than most other personality tests. The group form is less well studied but is probably better than any other group test because it includes scales designed to indicate lying or lack of understanding. The MMPI is a clinical instrument designed for use by clinical psychologists as a diagnostic tool for work with severely disturbed individuals. While it might be useful with exceptional students, it is not an instrument for routine school use and interpretation by school counselors.

The projective techniques for obtaining a picture of personality are among the most imaginative approaches to the study of people. The Rorschach, Thematic Apperception Test, Blacky

Pictures, Rosenzweig Picture-Frustration Study, and others are all interesting and intriguing approaches to personality. All are individual tests [13] and none produce numerical scores but are interpreted descriptively by the examiner. Much in the interpretation depends upon the orientation of the examiner and his approach to the particular techniques. The projective techniques do not lend themselves to statistical study although attempts have been made to establish validity and reliability for some of them. Despite considerable research, these tests cannot be said to have the statistical base that the objective measures have. In the hands of a sensitive trained clinician, these tests are both useful and interesting, but they are in no sense suitable instruments for school use.

The projective techniques offer one suggestion to the counselor who is contemplating the use of a personality inventory in his school. The varied results and widely differing interpretations obtained on the projective instruments lend credence to the idea that personality itself cannot be measured in the same way that other attributes are estimated. The answers to the questions, What kind of a person is he? and What makes him behave the way he does? may not lend themselves to numerical expression but rather require description and discussion in broader, less rigidly concrete terms. Pending further investigations, the counselor desiring to learn something about the personality of a student has no better source of information than the interview.

Uses and Abuses

Some of the uses and abuses of test data have already been discussed, but others not related to the inherent qualities of the tests deserve mention here. The good test suitably used and properly administered can supply the counselor with valuable

---

[13] A group form of the Rorschach is gaining in popularity in industrial personnel work. To date it has not been used in the schools and it never should be. It is a totally invalid test.

information about the individual, provided the counselor takes the precaution of regarding the data as an estimate rather than an exact quantity.

The current popularity of school testing programs stems in part from the prevailing faith in things scientific, for testing has a quality of appearing scientific. Testing has always come into prominence when large numbers of people have to be sorted out for some purpose and, with the increasing number of students, sorting has seemed necessary to some educators. The underwriting of testing programs under the National Defense Education Act has done nothing to decrease this popularity. Finally, the tendency of many school people to copy what is done in other systems has led to proliferation of testing without a sound reason for the program.

Perhaps the greatest single abuse of measurement is *purposeless testing*. A test should be given only for a good and sufficient reason: because it provides information obtainable in no other way; because it describes, within reasonable limits of accuracy, some facet of the individual; because it provides information more efficiently than other methods; because it most effectively implements the purposes of the educational process. The school counselor should administer tests for the purpose of advancing his understanding of the individual student and that student's understanding of himself. Viewed with the criterion of purpose in mind, most testing programs fall flat.

Tests are currently administered for a variety of reasons, most of which are neither good nor sufficient. The mere fact that a test is used in one school is no justification for its use in all schools. Counselors in small schools may not need the same kind of test data—or as much—as those in large schools. Part-time counselors may need more or fewer data, depending upon the amount of time they can devote to guidance. Each counselor should work out a testing program that helps him to fulfill the purposes of guidance in his school. Imitation is not a good and sufficient reason for testing.

Neither is the availability of federal money for testing a good and sufficient reason for doing it. The National Defense Education Act has made funds available to many schools that could not finance testing programs on limited budgets. These funds have enabled some counselors to do the testing that is really needed in their institutions. Nevertheless, unnecessary testing done because the money for materials is at hand is an unjustifiable misuse of school time and a waste of federal money that might better go to other uses.

Nor is curiosity a good and sufficient reason for testing. Some counselors seem to give tests just to find out what they will get as results. This curiosity is almost an unjustifiable prying into the personal worlds of individual students. A genuine research purpose, which might also be labeled curiosity, is a legitimate reason for testing, for only through research will tests improve. The prurient, probing curiosity that attaches itself to some kinds of testing, however, is perhaps the best reason for *not* testing.

The desire for completely filled cumulative records also leads to purposeless testing. While complete dossiers on every student may seem good in theory, they do not attest to the quality of the guidance program or its effectiveness. If tests are given and the results entered on the student's record, some further use should be made of the data either in promoting the student's academic progress or in aiding him toward greater self-understanding. Otherwise the time is wasted. Test results should be shared with teachers in such a way as to enhance the teacher's understanding of the students and his capacity for working with them. A frequent complaint from students is that they take tests and never hear any more about them. If testing is to fulfill its purpose, the results must be used for some legitimate educational endeavor.

In any discussion of the uses of tests, a distinction must be made between legitimate and reprehensible uses of test scores. Sharing IQ scores with professionally minded teachers who will utilize them to the advantage of the students is a legitimate use. Writing IQ scores on the class seating chart so that one's eye is inevitably caught and held by the minute and meaningless differences in scores is reprehensible. Labeling students in terms of their test scores is indefensible, and yet teachers and counselors continually allow themselves to be influenced by these estimates of the student's ability. The use of a personality inventory with an individual student as a focus for discussion in an interview might be quite legitimate, whereas the administration of a personality test for the purpose of selection would be a gross misuse of the test.

Essentially the use of tests imposes three responsibilities upon the counselor. First, he needs to be well acquainted with the test he proposes to use in order to know the purposes for which it was designed. Second, he must know the purposes for which he and the other members of the school staff want to use the test. If these two sets of purposes conflict, the test is being misused. And finally, the counselor has to insure that the test results are used in a manner consonant with the purposes. The basic consideration for the counselor should be: would he like his own test scores to be handled in the manner in which he contemplates handling those of his students? Many school testing practices would be outlawed if this simple evaluative criterion were applied more frequently.

Prehaps the most damaging abuse of testing is the incredibly *poor test interpretation* done in many schools. If counselors honestly believe that tests should help the student develop self-understanding, they must accept their responsibility for helping students to understand test results. Counselors should carry out this responsibility in such a way as to further the student's progress toward maturity and to enlarge his horizons for the future.

Unfortunately for counselors, the test interpretation interview provides an opportunity to meet many of their own personal needs: for displaying their knowledge of the subject, for being the authority, for appearing omnipotent, for impressing the student, and for justifying the judgments they feel obligated to give. The temptations offered in the test interpretation session are strong and counselors would not be human if they did not sometimes succumb to them. But test interpretation is part of

counseling and a counseling interview is not designed to permit
the counselor to deliver an erudite lecture or to impose his value
judgments upon his counselee. Counselor needs have no place
in any counseling session; student needs are and must remain
the focus.

Telling the student about his scores will have relatively little
meaning for him unless the discussion verges upon one of the
weaker areas of his self-concept and then the effect is likely to
be damaging to the student's ego structure. Telling is not an
effective method of conveying emotionally charged information.
Rather the student has to arrive at the point where he can accept
and internalize the information so completely that it becomes a
part of him and of all that makes him the individual he is.

Perhaps no area in counseling is more value laden than test
interpretation. High scores are "good" and low scores are "bad";
the "bright" boy is "admirable," the "dull" boy is "inconsequen-
tal"; the high achiever is a "hard worker," the underachiever is
"lazy"; the boy whose interests indicate he is heading for a socially acceptable area of work has "laudable ambition," the boy
who is still floundering is "indecisive"; the student who hides
his feelings about his test scores is "manly," the student who rejects the test findings is "immature." Test interpretation tends in
many instances to sound like a divine judgment. But counselors
are not measuring the length of a room or the amount of water
in a cup, they are discussing *estimates* of people's abilities and
these do not warrant judgments—only understanding and concern for how best to utilize them.

Counselor values are not the only ones involved in test interpretation. The student, too, judges himself in terms of his
scores often more harshly than the counselor would dare to do.
Part of test interpretation then becomes the process of helping
the student to temper his own judgments and to examine his
own values and their implications in his life. Here again it is
the student's values that are important and the counselor's values
that have no place in the process.

Group interpretation of tests is usually even more disastrous than the ordinary individual approach. The teacher or counselor attempting the interpretation cannot take into account all the feelings and values of thirty-odd students. In an attempt to handle an impossible situation, he is likely to become either so vague as to be unintelligible or so authoritarian as to eliminate discussion. In one instance of group interpretation of the Kuder, at least three-quarters of the students came away thinking that the Kuder measured their aptitudes, instead of inventorying their interests. As one student remarked, "Whatever it is, I ain' got much." All too often, this is the feeling that many students experience after these group sessions. Students are not, and should not be expected to be, experts in measurement. It is the counselor's responsibility to help the students to develop some comprehension of what their own scores mean.

Perhaps the most detrimental aspect of test interpretation is the limiting effect it can have upon the student's plans, aspirations, and view of himself. Attempts at prediction provide a good example of this delimiting procedure. In one school, all the tenth-grade students were given a modern language aptitude test. In a group counseling session, the students received their scores and a prediction table based upon the test scores and modern language grades attained by members of the class ahead of them. The students were then helped to predict their possible modern language grades from their test scores. At the same time, they were warned that the number represented in the prediction table was too small for accuracy. The experiment was considered successful because the students who had undergone this experience achieved somewhat higher grades in the subject when they finally took it. But what of the students who were scared away from taking a modern language by the inexact prediction based upon insufficient data obtained from essentially inaccurate measuring devices? Might not such a procedure as this indicate that the only important thing in a course is the grade one can expect to get?

Other tests can be and are used to delimit the student's aspirations and to circumscribe his horizons. Many youngsters know their limitations only too well. Parents, teachers, and counselors usually point them out all too frequently. Students are less sure of their abilities and assets and need to bolster their wavering self-confidence with whatever reinforcement they can get from tests. In recent years, most writers have emphasized the precept, "In test interpretation, start with the positive and work the discussion around to the less favorable." If one is to avoid limiting the student and reinforcing his own lack of self-esteem, that precept might better read, "Start with the student and allow him to work around to whatever he needs to discuss in terms of his test scores." If counselors could rid themselves of the ideas that the student is always ignorant and misinformed about himself and his potentialities and that test scores are always right, they might be better able to help the student to interpret tests in such a manner as to contribute to his further development.

One other abuse of testing has contributed greatly to the misuse and misinterpretation of the results. Educators, test publishers, various writers for the popular press, and lay critics of the schools have been guilty of drastically *overselling tests* to the general public. Tests simply cannot do all the things many people believe they can do. An intelligence test can give a rough estimate of a person's scholastic ability, but it cannot determine whether or how he will use that ability. Tests cannot select from a group of people the one most likely to be able to do a certain job well. And yet the general public thinks tests can do all these things and more. To insure appropriate use of test results, educators and laymen need re-education as to what can be expected of tests and how results can best be handled for the benefit of the individual student.

For the counselor, the most frequent abuse of measurement stems from the overuse of the profile sheet and might be called *test profile counseling*. The counselor whose testing program is elaborate and whose cumulative records are detailed, all too often finds himself thinking in terms of profiles and test scores rather than in terms of the human being. Test scores do not equal the person and they never will, but the tendency is to lose the person somewhere in the peaks and valleys of the neatly drawn profile. Counselors who love measurement and dislike talking with students are all too common. They are the foremost practitioners of test profile counseling. Somehow in the process of trying to turn the student into a set of numbers, they lose sight of the essential humanity of the person behind the scores. Such a process ceases to be counseling and becomes judgment.

Summary

Thanks to methodological theory which attempts to relate "facts" about the individual and "facts" about occupations to produce a reasoned occupational choice, testing is currently much in fashion in vocational guidance. Test scores have a spurious appearance of being "facts" and yet they are not. Test scores are only estimates of what a person can do on a limited set of tasks at a given time under a particular set of circumstances. Another time, a different set of tasks, and an altered set of circumstances produce different scores often having little relationship to previous set. And yet, test scores are the "facts" upon which methodological theorists would have students base their vocational decisions. This reliance upon test scores has led to the development of the myths that man can be measured and that those measurements have implications for his success in his education and vocation.

Chapter 3

CLASSIFICATION SYSTEMS

NOTHING IS more confusing to the school counselor than the classification of occupational information. He sees no way out of the jungle of occupational brochures and pamphlets other than organizing them in some fashion. He may try to set up a complete file according to some formal system and then to teach that system to his teachers and students. On the other hand, he may buy a filing system and teach that method to his teachers and students. Then again, he may declare that the filing of occupational information is the librarian's job and leave it to her. The counselor may even deposit the brochures in the wastebasket and turn his attention elsewhere. Whatever his solution, filing poses a continual, unsolvable problem, for occupational information continues to accumulate.

Some of the confusion arises because classification systems are rarely studied and discussed from the point of view of the school counselor using them. The weaknesses, strengths, and uses of each system are not related to the schools or the students for whose benefit they are presumably established. Rather, systems are reviewed in isolation or from the point of view of the theorists formulating them.

The multiplicity of classification systems is another source of difficulty for the counselor and his students. The counselor may file information according to a formal system and yet speak and act in terms of less formal systems. The result for everyone is confusion engendered by the myth that a single classification system is working within the school. Within any school two kinds of occupational classification exist—the covert informal and the overt formal systems.

Informal Systems

Any counselor working in a school offering separate academic and vocational curricula faces an occupational classification system inherent in this division. Often the counselor's *raison d'être*, particularly in the junior high shool, is to help students make wise curricular choices. These choices are essentially basic occupational decisions.

Logically, the counselor could adapt this curricular structure to his occupational information and divide it under *academic* or *vocational* headings. Such a division would reflect the immediate concern of every student, for it is most closely related to the first important vocational decision each must make.

Theoretically, students may switch curricula and some, but not many, do. The gifted athlete may be lured into the academic with the offer of college scholarships; the late maturing student may suddenly find his interests changing; the emotionally troubled student may gain new perspectives and insight, and the student with learning or cultural handicaps may remedy his weaknesses. These students, however, are exceptions because all too often the first major decision is irrevocable.

Why then does a school counselor hesitate to use a curricular classification? In filing thousands of occupational brochures the counselor often finds it difficult to establish subheads under the major headings. Should he use a simple alphabetical system within the divisions academic and vocational? Immediately the complexities multiply. Is Chemical Engineer filed under C or E or cross-indexed? Where would a student hunt for information about maintenance jobs? Under Building Superintendent, Maintenance Engineer, or any of the other, often euphemistic, titles ssigned? And should Maintenance Engineer be included in the general category of Engineer?

One alternative might be to group the jobs by the amount of education required, but educational requirements can also be ticklish. Where, for example, should the counselor file Professional Baseball Player or Professional Football Player? The baseball player might or might not find college a necessity. The football player almost always finds the minor leagues of college football a requirement, although occasionally a "Big Daddy" Lipscomb can hop from the sand lots to the major leagues without a college education. The educational requirements of occupations do not furnish the counselor with workable subheads for his filing system.

The academic–vocational divisions of occupational materials leave the counselor with no readily apparent subdivisions under those main headings. Faced with seemingly endless decisions, he turns to other classification systems in his efforts to reduce the chaos.

Another occupational classification that students meet in their social studies classes, their sociology textbooks, and the daily newspaper consists of the *professional, white-collar* and *blue-collar* groupings. This terminology is familiar to everyone. These three divisions have become a status hierarchy. Counselors as well as students and parents are conscious of the status implied in the word Professional.

No school counselor groups occupational information by this system—the one actually taught in the schools. Perhaps he hesitates to make decisions about the status of various occupations. Perhaps the difficulties of classification baffle him. What actually is a profession? Where should he file Actress, Mortician, or the previously troubling Professional Football Player and Maintenance Engineer? The counselor might view such a classification system as too difficult and turn to one requiring fewer value judgments. And yet, many students tell the counselor that they want to go into one of the professions." Not many students could compile a list of even ten professions; most of them hesitate after doctor, lawyer, and the newest addition, research scientist. If the gaining of professional status is of primary importance to students, a classification system of occupations in these familiar terms might be useful. The counselor balks, however, at the problems of classification and ignores this tripartite division.

Another informal system of classifying occupational information is by *subject matter*. The counselor frequently turns to subject matter when he tries to discover where a student's interests lie. Teachers and parents also talk about youngsters' being good or bad in subject categories such as English, science, or mathematics. Teachers phrase most of their vocational advice in terms of subjects: "You should go on in English. You're good at it." Students themselves use subject-matter classifications as a framework for analysis of their own inclinations, preferences, and abilities.

Rare, however, is the school in which occupational information is classified according to subject matter. The student interested in literature has to learn how to use a formal system of classification in order to find out what occupations match his interests. Many teachers and counselors are not much help because they too must first cross the barrier of a filing system.

The reasons for not using a subject-matter classification for the actual filing of occupational materials are difficult to establish. Perhaps counselors do not view it as formally acceptable. Textbooks on occupational information give little or no attention to this indigenous school system. Many counselors feel that such a classification is too difficult because the old problem of subheads rises to haunt them. Yet a subject-matter system might be the most meaningful to the students using it.

Whereas students and teachers most frequently think in terms of subject matter, the counselor himself discusses occupations under still other headings. His covert system consists of the occupational groupings established by *interest inventories*. If he uses the Kuder Preference Record, he discusses occupations with students in terms of Mechanical, Computational, Scientific, Pe suasive, Artistic, Literary, Musical, Social Service, Clerical, and Outdoor interests. If the counselor administers the Thurstone Interest Schedule, he uses the interest groupings of Physical Science, Biological Science, Computational, Business, Executive, Persuasive, Linguistic, Humanitarian, Artistic, and Musical. If the counselor works at the college level, he will probably talk in terms of the specific occupations on the Strong Vocational Interest Blank. More likely than not, he will ignore the broad groupings discussed in the manual and use the fifty or so occupations listed on the profile sheet, such as Group I: Artist, Psychologist, Architect, Physician, Dentist, Osteopath, and Veterinarian. The counselor's mental classification of occupations parallels that of the particular interest inventory he administers. Interest inventories and the classification systems they suggest are the most pervasive in use today.

Suppose a counselor uses the Kuder classifications in talking with a student. The student is likely to ask what occupations are suggested by the interest categories in which he scored high. The counselor will probably name several and then use the Kuder manual, in which a few occupations are grouped under the headings used in scoring the inventory. The test manual actually lists less than 2 per cent of the total number of occupations. For additional information, both the student and the counselor must turn to a different classification, one to which the Kuder system is not applicable! To be consistent, the counselor relying upon the questionable Kuder should classify his occupational information according to its categories; otherwise the student's horizons are limited by the few and specific occupations listed in the Kuder manual.

The Strong Vocational Interest Blank limits even more stringently both the student and the counselor. The profile sheet lists about 50 specific occupations for men and only twenty-six for women. The Strong VIB leads both the student and the counselor to think in terms of the listed occupations. Since the Strong list is empirically derived, it can be expanded only by further experimentation. If the counselor were to classify occupational materials according to the Strong, his files would necessarily include information on only 50 occupations for men and 26 for women. Any system based on the Strong would be self-limiting.

Occupational classifications based on interests vary with the inventories used. In general, they are extremely limiting and do little to clarify occupational groupings. They simply add another covert system to those already present in the school.

Every school system also contains *library* classifications of occupational information. The librarian classifies the occupational materials she handles according to the Dewey Decimal System, the Library of Congress catalog card numbers, or some idiosyncratic system. Invariably the library system is used in conjunction with some other method of classification of occupational information. Novels, biographies, autobiographies, and other nonfiction contain valuable and lively occupational information. These books are in the library. Regardless of the formal classification system used by the counselor, it is supplementary to that of the library.

The informal classification systems (academic–vocational; professional, white-collar, blue-collar; subject matter; interest; and library) are endemic in every school. They exist whether diagnosed or not. They are not necessarily compatible with each other. They are even less likely to be compatible with the formal classification systems the school counselor adds to them.

Formal Systems

The school counselor apparently accepts the myth that occupational information can be meaningfully filed according to a single formal system. He safeguards his acceptance of the myth by assuming that his formal system is understood and used exclusively throughout the school. The counselor soothes whatever doubts he has about the success of his formal system by frequent explanations of it to teachers and students, usually through printed guides and lectures. He can then feel somewhat assured that everyone has adopted his formal system. Perhaps he can even "con" himself into believing that he uses it.

Actually the counselor is caught in a conflict. Methodological theory dictates that he be an informational expert and have as much material as possible at his finger tips. The only way he can fill this prescribed role is to have a "complete" filing system and the most "complete" systems are the most formal. They are also the most complex and the least familiar. Essentially, the emphasis on information and its availability to the counselor has given rise to the law of affinity: the more formal and complex the filing system, the nearer the files will move to the counselor's desk.

The counselor realizes that formal systems tend to separate the students from the information, but often he sees no way of preventing this separation. Accrediting associations evaluate his program by the completeness of his formal informational files. State departments of education recommend that he use a formal system, usually that of the *Dictionary of Occupational Titles*. Many pressures combine to force him into the role of informational expert, with complete inviolate files classifying occupational information in some formal way. Quelling his own doubts about their usefulness for students, the counselor makes his choice among the formal systems discussed and recommended in his textbooks or by outside agencies.

One formal system, closely allied to the status classification discussed earlier, is an integral part of occupational information itself and of many counselors' classifications of it. In seeking a synthesis of past census data, Alba M. Edwards [1] arrived at a socioeconomic scale of occupations consisting of Professional, Proprietary and Managerial, Clerical and Sales, Skilled and Supervisory, Semi-skilled, and Unskilled. Most, if not all, of the divisions of the Edwards Scale find a place in other classification systems. The counselor often uses it for subdivisions. He may, for example, have a major heading like "Aviation" or "Medicine," and file occupations under that heading according to the Ed-

[1] See *Population. Comparative Occupation Statistics for the United States, 1870 to 1940* (Sixteenth Census of the United States: 1940, Washington, United States Government Printing Office, 1943).

wards Scale. Needless to say, this scale has all the weaknesses of any status classification.

Most counselors eventually adopt classification systems used by various government departments. Even within this framework the counselor has a wide choice, for rarely do two government departments use the same system. Since each department serves a special purpose, each uses a system designed to implement its particular purpose. The differences in the systems used often account for discrepancies among governmental reports, for conclusions are based upon varying groupings of numbers. Hence the school counselor must view with care the primary purpose of all governmental systems before he adopts one particular classification.

The Bureau of the Census, for example, deals almost exclusively with numbers. It issues reports about the population of the United States and the distribution of that population according to such breakdowns as sex, age, location, and occupation. It also offers a revised two-dimensional numerical classification under the major headings, industry and occupation. Each major group has a three-digit numerical code, an alphabetical code, or both—a system as easily assimilated as the numbers used in the DOT. The indexing structure for the industries is:

Code	*Major Industry Group*
A, and 017 and 018	Agriculture, forestry, and fisheries
126 to 156	Mining
C	Construction
B, M, and 2-, 3-, 4-	Manufacturing
L, and 5-	Transportation, communication, and other public utilities
D, F, G, and 606 to 696	Wholesale and retail trade
7-	Finance, insurance, and real estate
806 to 809	Business and repair service
K, and 826 to 839	Personal services
846 to 849	Entertainment and recreation services
E, H, and 867 to 898	Professional and related services
J, and 906 to 936	Public administration

The breakdowns under these headings include 149 industries.

The second half of the code deals with the occupational classification, in which "296 occupation categories" are distinguished. "An occupation category consists of a group of related occupation titles, which, in effect, define a particular field of work." [2] The major grouping is as follows:

Code	Major Occupation Group
0- and 1-	Professional, technical, and kindred workers
N, and 222	Farmers and farm managers
R, and 250 to 285	Managers, officials, and proprietors, excluding farm
Y, Z, and 301 to 360	Clerical and kindred workers
S, and 380 to 395	Sales workers
Q, and 401 to 555	Craftsmen, foremen, and kindred workers
T, W, and 601 to 721	Operatives and kindred workers
P, and 801 to 803	Private household workers
810 to 890	Service workers, except private household
U, V, and 901 and 905	Farm laborers and foremen
X, and 960 to 973	Laborers, except farm and mine

These two codes can then be combined to index occupation categories within industries except for the non-industrial occupations which will naturally have only the single code. The system is derived from census reports and reviews of other systems.

According to the same logic that underlies the adoption of other formal systems of classification, the school counselor could use the census system. He does use it when he attempts to identify labor trends and population changes. Usually, however, he speaks about employment trends in terms of the census system but uses another, equally complex system in dealing with his own informational materials.

---

[2] *Alphabetical Index of Occupations and Titles* (1960 Census of Population, Washington, United States Department of Commerce, Bureau of the Census, 1960), p. viii.

Some school counselors adopt the Standard Industrial Classification used by the Bureau of the Budget. This contains nine major categories—Agriculture, Forestry, Fisheries; Mining; Construction; Manufacturing; Wholesale and Retail Trade; Finance, Insurance, and Real Estate; Transportation and Communication; Services; Government—which are subdivided first into 91 groups, then into 519 related industries, and finally into 1,530 separate industries. Widespread use has stilled objections to the logic of some of the combinations in the categories. Students who wish to find out about careers in such industries as coal mining or heavy construction can seek information through this industrial classification. Volumes I and II of the *Standard Industrial Classification Manual* supply the counselor with the essential knowledge for setting up such a system scientifically.

Actually there is as much justification for using an industrial classification system within the schools as there is for using the one that is most rapidly being adopted. Popular usage has made the system described in Volume II of the *Dictionary of Occupational Titles* (DOT) a must for all schools. Because of its omnipresence, a more detailed look at the purposes and structure of the DOT classification is necessary.

The multi-volume *Dictionary of Occupational Titles,* first published in 1939 and revised in 1949, is the work of the United States Employment Service of the Department of Labor. The DOT is the most complete listing of occupations ever devised and the most detailed system of classifying that information Its original purpose was to inform people working in the USES about the vast varieties of occupations. These volumes afforded a quick standard means of analyzing an applicant's previous employment record and, on the basis of his experience, finding a suitable job for him.

The first volume of the DOT contains an alphabetical listing of job titles, with some descriptive information under each major title. The second volume assigns classification numbers to jobs in a set pattern. The 1949 revision, the one used in most schools, contains in these first two volumes 40,023 listings of occupations.

Practice makes the numerical classification system easier, but it remains complex to the uninitiated despite Robert Hoppock's optimistic statement that it is "very simple when once explained."[3] Basically, the DOT classification is a series of numbers running as high as five or six digits. The first digit is the major occupational group and each following digit represents further divisions within that group.[4] Physician, for example, is listed in Volume I in this manner: "PHYSICIAN (medical ser.) 0–26.10." The first digit (0) signifies the "Professional and

[3] Robert Hoppock, *Occupational Information* (New York, McGraw-Hill, 1957), p. 48.

[4] See *Dictionary of Occupational Titles,* Volumes I, II, and IV, (United States Department of Labor, Washington, Government Printing Office, 1949). In Volume II, page ix, there is a brief outline of the structure:

0– Professional and Managerial Occupations
    0–0 through 0–3 Professional Occupations
    0–4 through 0–6 Semi-Professional Occupations
    0–7 through 0–9 Managerial and Official Occupations
1– Clerical and Sales Occupations
    1–0 through 1–4 Clerical and kindred Occupations
    1–5 through 1–9 Sales and kindred Occupations
2– Service Occupations
    2–0 through 2–1 Domestic Service Occupations
    2–2 through 2–5 Personal Service Occupations
    2–6 through 2–7 Protective Service Occupations
    2–8 through 2–9 Building Service Workers and Porters
3– Agriculture, Fishery, Forestry, and Kindred Occupations
    3–0 through 3–4 Agricultural, Horicultural, and kindred Occupations
    3–8 Fishery Occupations
    3–9 Forestry (except logging), and Hunting and Trapping Occupations
4– and 5– Skilled Occupations
6– and 7– Semiskilled Occupations
8– and 9– Unskilled Occupations

The total lack of consistency between and within categories is readily apparent.

Managerial" group of occupations and the second digit (2), a professional occupation within that group. Each digit has a meaning, and the DOT contains complete explanations of the use of the numbers. There are also printed guides available to aid the user. Since the numbers may run as high as six digits, as "WERNER-PLEIDERER-MIXER OPERATOR (roof materials) 6–56.610," constant referral to explanatory materials is necessary. Some vocational counselors after prolonged use of the system learn to think in terms of it and can carry on "numerical conversations" when discussing the more familiar occupations.

By means of its numerical system, the DOT identifies job families. The first three digits denote the family of related occupations. The structure of these job families can be seen through following an example of the cross-indexing within Volume I. Suppose a student were seeking information about the work of a bouncer. He might look in the alphabetically arranged Volume I and find the listing: "BOUNCER (amuse. & rec.) *see* FLOORMAN I *under* DETECTIVE II (any ind.)." [5] Following these directions, he would find that "DETECTIVE (any ind.) II" also contains the number "2–65.02," indicating that the occupation belongs to the service group, 2, and the "Protective Service Occupations," 6, in that group. He would also find that the

DETECTIVE (any ind.) II.2–65.02. Polices the premises of a private business establishment to preserve order, and maintain the standards of behavior established by that organization.

Continuing his search under this main heading, he would look for "FLOORMAN I" and discover "bouncer":

FLOORMAN (amuse. & rec.) I bouncer; house detective; houseman. Patrols a place of entertainment, circulating among patrons to prevent improper dancing, skating, or similar activities, and to detect persons annoying other patrons or damaging furnishings of estab-

[5] Most students would probably stop at this point unless fulfilling a specific assignment. Some curious students might investigate the system once to find out how it works. Incidentally, the style of writing in the DOT excerpts is typical of that used in most governmental occupational information pamphlets.

lishment. Warns persons guilty of these infractions and if they become obstreperous removes them tactfully from establishment, but uses force if necessary. May call police if unable to quell disturbance.

By this time, the student has found that the work of the bouncer is closely related to the work of the floorman, house detective, and houseman, and similar to the work of detectives (any ind.). Looking in the school files under 2–65.02, the student may find further information about these jobs and know that all information grouped under 2–65 will pertain to related occupations. Hence he may browse and perhaps find an occupation such as floorman or houseman that he never knew was related to bouncer.

Despite the difficulties the DOT poses for students, it is the most popular classification system for counselors. Increasingly, state departments of education are recommending its use. Especially important in explaining the DOT's popularity, however, is the fact noted by Hoppock—that it causes the *counselor* fewer problems: "40,023 decisions have already been made for him. . . . The counselor will find that he still has some decisions to make himself, but not so many as with any other system." [6]

Even more subtle are the unnoted reasons for the use of the DOT. The system appears to be scientific and demands expertness from the counselor. He can feel secure in the knowledge that he has 40,023 occupations at his finger tips. It is interesting that all discussions of the DOT classification system fail to mention the student. Rather it is discussed from the counselor's point of view as though he, and not the student, were the one to use the information.

The weaknesses of the DOT are many. First, it was designed for use by experts in employment offices, not for students in schools. Its use creates copious files of occupational information within a counselor's office. These files separate the student from the information, but then the original purpose of the DOT was to fill an expert's needs. Any school counselor using the DOT

---

[6] *Occupational Information,* p. 49.

as his basis for filing has, in concentrating upon his own needs, automatically forgotten the students and the real purpose of occupational information—student exploration.

The second major weakness is inherent in the system itself, for the DOT is not a particularly good grouping of occupations. Filing decisions may be made for the counselor, but they are made in terms of an inconsistent and faulty system. The major groupings of the DOT are themselves a mixture: Professional and Managerial; Clerical and Sales; Service; Agriculture, Fishery, and Forestry; Skilled; Semiskilled; and Unskilled. In part, the groups are the familiar socioeconomic ones with the addition of one industrial (Agriculture, Fishery, and Forestry) and two (Clerical and Sales, Service) dealing with the types of work. The subdivisions in each category follow no set scheme and are even more of a hodgepodge. The DOT is simultaneously the most formal and complete classification of occupations and the most confusing. It has no apparent rationale.

Many of those who acknowledge these weaknesses in the DOT, still defend it because of the job families it establishes. Herein, however, lies the third major weakness. Research is just beginning on the delineation of true job families, which are simple, interrelated occupations. At this point no one is certain what aspects of occupations are the most important in the process of interrelating them. And yet the DOT classification establishes job families within the framework of a mixed-up classification system without a rationale.

Except that the DOT seems to meet the personal needs of the counselor, there is absolutely no justification for using it in the schools. The inherent weaknesses in the system itself should make counselors question it, but many are unwilling to do so. The only school purpose it serves is to make the counselor a specious occupational expert.

Difficulties with the DOT have given rise to the sale of commercial filing systems, most of which are watered-down versions of the DOT, obviously designed for counselors who have not had sufficient graduate work on the original system. Sales must be good, because more of these commercial systems are appearing on the market. Basically they are a waste of school money, as are the occupational pamphlets that are often sold with them.

Within the past five years, pattern theorists have begun to examine the classifications of occupations. These investigations were stimulated by Roe, who found that the available systems were useless for her particular purpose of relating occupational choice and personality. She claimed that such formal systems as the DOT and the Census were not "of much value psychologically, nor can they be adapted to any psychological interpretation. They have little relation to personal requirements, and very little relation to interests."[7] Roe's statements about the *purposes* of classification systems stand as a landmark in counseling literature. They represent the first thorough questioning of the utility of current classification systems.

For her purpose of relating occupations and personality, Roe set up a two-way classification system composed of Groups and Levels of occupations. The Groups—Service, Business Contact, Organization, Technology, Outdoor, Science, and General Cultural—are classification by the "primary focus of the activity." The Levels—Professional and Managerial 1; Professional and Managerial 2; Semi-Professional and Small Business; Skilled; Semi-Skilled; and Unskilled—are classifications "based upon degrees of responsibility, capacity, and skill," which Roe carefully points out may not be "three exactly correlated" entities.[8] Roe's system is one of the most consistent currently available.

Roe not only presents a rationale for her particular classification but also summarizes the psychological knowledge (or lack of it) about the occupations within each category and points out the types of research needed. Vocational experts have given some attention to Roe's classification system and have discussed whether or not it might be more suitable for school use than the DOT. They have practically ignored the many questions Roe

[7] Anne Roe, *The Psychology of Occupations* (New York, John Wiley, 1956), p. 144.
[8] *Ibid.*, pp. 145–50.

raises about the purposes of such systems and the psychological factors involved in the various occupations. In so doing, they have overlooked much of value in Roe's work.

At about the same time that Roe was devising a classification system adapted to her work, Super was seeking one that would suit his research purpose in the Career Pattern Study. He found that he could not use the DOT so he adapted Roe's system, adding to it a third dimension "enterprise" composed of the following categories: Agriculture-Forestry; Mining; Construction; Manufacture; Trade; Finance; Transport; Services; and Government.[9] Reports from the Career Pattern Study, which are only now beginning to appear,[10] will determine the usefulness of Super's system for his research purpose.

In combination, these two theorists have raised the most vital question concerning classification systems: Can a system set up to serve one purpose adequately serve another, entirely different purpose?

It is interesting that Super, who finds the DOT inadequate for his research purpose, seems to accept unquestioningly the school use of the DOT, although he carefully points out the weaknesses in the system itself and calls it a "confused mixture." [11] The work of Super and Roe, however, may point the way to real examination of the systems now being used and their purposes.

Whatever formal classification system the counselor selects, he still runs into difficulties. He has added another system to those already present in the school. In adopting a governmental

[9] Donald Super, *The Psychology of Careers* (New York, Harper, 1957), pp. 46–51.

[10] These reports are published by the Bureau of Publications, Teachers College, Columbia University. The first report, *Vocational Development, A Framework for Research* (1957), deals with the background of the study; the second, *The Vocational Maturity of Ninth-Grade Boys* (1960), presents early findings. Both are essential reading for counselors.

[11] *The Psychology of Careers*, p. 49. Super states that the DOT is "a useful tool for organizing and making a vast fund of information useful to vocational counselors, manpower specialists, placement officers, and entrants into the labor market." (p. 46) His list does not include students, except for those who might fall into the category of "entrants."

method, he is changing the purpose for which the system was designed without examining that original purpose. Many counselors fail to recognize the weaknesses inherent in the governmental classifications.

The Need

The myth that the currently available filing systems are applicable to schools has blocked investigations into the usefulness of these systems for the student. Throughout the development of vocational guidance no one has proposed a method of dealing with occupational information that starts with the school and the student. The vested interests in the myth are too powerful and uncritical.

Increasingly within the past decade, the vise in which the counselor is trapped has tightened. Every day more counselors are being pressured to adopt formal filing methods. The only possible breakthrough is a thorough examination of the myths of methodological theory and classification systems. As long as these myths remain, the counselor will continue to find that the formal classification systems imposed upon him keep his students away from occupational information.

Chapter 4

INFORMATION

A POPULAR fallacious assumption is that the primary purpose of education is the teaching of facts. Parents ask their children, "What did you learn in school today?" An answer in specifics such as "A new song" or "Ten new words" or "How to work quadratic equations" meets with approval. The great appeal of television quiz shows is another aspect of this assumption. Many parents even required their children to watch these programs because they were "educational," the premise presumably being that facts once heard would be retained. The increasing use of objective tests of all kinds has done much to further among professional educators as well as parents this conception of education as memorizing facts.

An accompanying assumption is that education takes place only within the school and through the use of such formal materials as textbooks designed for that purpose. For example, the youngster putting together his "ham" radio set will be told to stop wasting his time and to do his science homework. The teen-ager reading for enjoyment a novel, biography, or even an unassigned Shakespearean play will hear, "Get your nose out of that book and get busy. How do you ever expect to learn anything?" Often the youngster who has learned to read on his own before entering school has to be taught formally to do it "right." In much the same way, employers judge the knowledge and learnings of applicants in terms of the formal courses they have taken. Learning and education are assumed to be institutionalized formal activities.

Small wonder then that the school counselor setting up an occupational information program for students tends to think in terms of these two assumptions. He views occupational information primarily as the "facts" contained in the pamphlets and brochures in his files, and educational information as the "facts" bound into college or vocational school catalogues and scholarship booklets. He also assumes that the students assimilate this "factual" information. He plans his programs without asking the fundamental questions, What is information? What is its purpose? Does it do what it is supposed to do?

The Nature of Information

Actually, information is everywhere and anywhere. It comes in all shapes, sizes, and forms. It is disseminated through all media, animate and inanimate. It enters through all the senses.

To each person, information is what he assimilates from the total of his own experiences, including the formal ones labeled "education." He selects and retains what is important to him from sources to which he is receptive. His own needs, feelings, intelligence, personality, and being determine his receptivity, perceptions, and selective processes. He learns as a result of everything to which he is exposed, and what precisely he learns from any exposure is determined by the person he is at that time.

Occupational learnings begin early and continue throughout a person's lifetime. The young child makes an early "occupational" grouping in terms of his own parents. His mother does certain things for and with him; his father does others. Either parent may be absent at certain times because of "work" obligations. The child begins to assimilate the idea that different people do different things as he meets the milkman, the grocer, the policeman, the carpenter, the doctor, the plumber—all the host of people doing a variety of things which he can observe. Interestingly enough, he is less likely to *observe* what his own father does, and unless his father's work coincides with his own observations he will be vague about it.

The child's experience is broadened through additional sources of information: the television programs he views, the pictures he sees in books, the stories he reads himself or has read to him, the adult conversations he partially understands, the people with whom he talks, and the games he plays. From these sources the child internalizes the information in terms of his own perceptions and experiential background. Lacking some or all of these informational sources, he will have a narrower base from which to start his own occupational explorations.

The basic process of internalizing occupational information does not change. Most adolescents have broadened their horizons and actually tried out different types of "work" at home or in school or through part-time employment, but this work experience supplements rather than supersedes the internalization process. The people in various jobs and the teen-ager's interaction with them continue to influence his perceptions and learnings. What he sees, feels, and experiences; the characters in stories or on television with whom he identifies; the mental pictures of various types of work he creates—all continue to be his most meaningful sources of occupational information. The adolescent becomes more aware of the externals of his parents' work, particularly of working hours, prestige, status, independence, and monetary returns. From his parents and the other significant adults in his life, he develops attitudes, feelings, and values about work. These learnings are often in conflict and differ sharply from the attitudes and values of his peers.

The same fundamental process of internalizing occupational information continues throughout a person's lifetime. The mental picture of what a secretary, a doctor, an insurance salesman, or a banker does arises out of a person's perceptions of his experiences with these people. The person living in a small town envisions the banker either as the teller with whom he deals or as the financial tycoon he sees portrayed on television. From the information most meaningful to him, each individual creates his picture, erroneous or not, of the worker and the occupation. His concept of training, salary, duties, way of life, and working conditions arises out of this composite of information, experience, misinformation, wish fulfillment, and fantasy.

This point of view toward information is extremely important for the school counselor too, for he views information from the starting point of his own experiences and internalizations. The status of any job is "high" or "low," the working conditions are "good" or "bad," the salary is "large" or "small," the work "interesting" or "dull" only from the point of reference of himself, his own job, and his background. The "facts" in occupational brochures are meaningful to student and to counselor only in terms of where each is at a given point in time.

What, then, is occupational information? Officially within a school program it is an amalgam of textbooks; outside readings; visits to businesses and industries; studies of occupations directly and indirectly in the classroom; motion pictures showing different jobs; formal occupational brochures, posters, and other materials; publications about educational opportunities ranging from college catalogues to picture booklets; assigned interviews with various workers; and college and career nights.

In many, if not most, school programs, information is viewed in even narrower terms. In the opinion of some counselors, occupational information is presented only in the classic pamphlet or brochure outlined by Parsons—the usual publication that deals with the work activities, work conditions, requirements for employment, personal qualifications, salary, chances for advancement, and the future of the specific occupation.[1] College infor-

---

[1] See discussion of Parsons' theory in Chapter I. The knowledge about the world of work that Parsons deemed essential became the structure of the occupational brochure (item 2 of his "three broad factors"). The current outline for the brochure closely resembles Parsons' suggestions and may be found in any book on occupational information or any pronouncement of the National Vocational Guidance Association. Perhaps information experts should keep in mind the comment of Montaigne: "The oldest and best known evil was ever more supportable than the one that was new and untried."

mation is the catalogue and often primarily the sections of that catalogue dealing with entrance requirements and scholarships available.

Unofficially, occupational information is a significant blending of daily observation; reading of all types; television and radio programs; motion pictures; interaction with various people; information from people ranging from peers to parents to strangers —all the cumulative learnings. The formal list is more specific, but the informal list is more important. The informal list includes the total of the person's existence.

Purpose and Accomplishment

The traditional purpose of formal programs of occupational information derives from methodological theory. Any writings from the time of Parsons to the present contain similar statements of purpose. In general, this aim is twofold: to acquaint the student with a variety of occupations and to furnish him with authentic, realistic, factual information about specific occupations.

"Authentic," "realistic," and "factual" are impressive adjectives. They somehow place the noun they modify beyond question. Reverence for these three adjectives has precluded the basic consideration: Is such formal information actually authentic, realistic, and factual? Can it ever be so?

Many modern books on occupational information warn the counselor against the use of inaccurate, outdated, and ill-written occupational materials. The National Vocational Guidance Association provides check lists for the counselor so that he can judge readily whether informational brochures are good or bad. These authorities eschew, however, the fundamental problems that arise from terminology, national coverage, change, the unknowns, and student motivation.

TERMINOLOGY. The vocabulary of occupational information and vocational guidance is deceptively simple. The common words are used everyday by millions of people who are certain they know the meanings of the terms. Its nouns are commonplace: work, leisure, career, job, position, occupation, vocation, avocation, working day, salary, wages, success, satisfaction, interests, intelligence, status, social class, entrance, preparation, stability, business, industry, choice, advancement, mobility, profession, and the titles of specific types of work, as well as some more technical (but still familiar) terms such as job classifications, job descriptions, and job analyses. The adjectives used in occupational materials are abstract—dull, challenging, routine, large, small, enviable, good, bad, and many other value-laden words.

If one were to stand on a street corner and ask a passerby whether he knows what the word "work" means, he would undoubtedly laugh at the question. Of course he knows! Furthermore, he engages in some form of it everyday. He pictures "work" from the starting point of his own experiences combined with his personal and societal system of values. Regardless of his "work," the passerby probably views himself as one of the hardest working persons in his immediate circle, or he has ready socially acceptable reasons for not filling that role. The long Puritan tradition still influences our culture with the concept that work, whatever it may be, is "good" and idleness is "bad" —a simple value judgment.

If one pursues the topic, he will find the passerby immediately establishing a variety of individualistic divisions concerning "work." He is very likely to compare easy and hard work, physical and mental work, outside and indoor work, dirty and clean work, and work itself with fun and enjoyment. Combinations of these comparisons are each person's idiosyncratic system of classifying work.

Even the single word "work" can have degrees of meaning. Personal values and experiences are the chief framers of the view of work that each person holds. They become so integrated with the word itself that divorce is impossible. One day Martha, the cleaning woman, found her writer-employer washing the

garbage pail and commented, "Oh, you're working." The writer
replied, "But I'm working when I'm writing." Martha made the
distinction, "Yes, I know, but today you're *really* working."

Experts in occupations face the same difficulties. Long usage
of words, impregnated with values, colors and shades precise
meanings. What work means to one person, it may not to another. Routine work to one person may be challenging to another. Some people view working a set number of hours in a
specific place as confining; others, as pleasurably secure. Even
a word such as "professional" causes disagreement. Is the professional athlete as professional as the professional lawyer? What
about the actor, mortician, teacher? Which is a professional and
why? The answer will be phrased in terms of the perspective
and values of the person replying. And experts have as many
answers as laymen.

Many books on occupational information or vocational guidance start with careful definitions of such terms as "work" and
"occupation." [2] Authors try to use these troubling words pre-

[2] There are as many definitions of the word "work" as there are authors writing about it. The great number of definitions point up the
difficulty everyone has in using the word in any but an individualistic
sense. At least we challenge any reader to keep in mind the author's
precise meaning of the term in reading any book! Many modern writers
on occupations, such as Hoppock and Baer and Roeber, have apparently
foregone any attempt to define the word.

The word "occupation" poses no fewer problems. Apparently, the
most popular technical definition is that supplied by C. L. Shartle (*Occupational Information,* New York, Prentice-Hall, 1952, pp. 25–26.
Shartle uses the same definitions in the revision, 1959), as he distin-
guishes among "occupation," "job," and "position." He maintains that
"vocation" is synonymous with "occupation" and offers these definitions:

Occupation: a group of similar jobs found in several establishments.
Job: a group of similar positions in one plant, business, institution, or
    other workplace.
Position: a set of tasks performed by one person.

Anne Roe takes issue with the Shartle definition of occupation and offers
one of her own: ". . . whatever an adult spends most of his time doing.
That may be what he does to earn a living or it may not." (*Psychology
of Occupations,* p. 3.)

cisely, but sooner or later connotations sneak into the denotations. Moreover, the reader brings with him his own set of interpretations, values, and meanings which obfuscate the author's definitions and intentions. Already the precision of terminology is lost.

Difficulties in terminology pose far more problems for students than for their counselors. Some school counselors are conscious of the problems in this area, whereas students are not. Students apply their own meanings and interpretations, often without realizing that their views do not coincide with those of the writer, the counselor, or other adults. Can information expressed in value-ridden terms be "authentic" and "factual"?

NATIONAL COVERAGE. The popular outline for the brief informational tract proposed by Parsons was developed on the basis of experience in only one city, Boston. Later, informational experts adopted the outline for use in brochures and monographs that would have national coverage. Immediately they increased the problems inherent in their task.

The nature of the difficulties in writing an occupational brochure that is national in scope can be seen even in one of the most standardized occupations, medicine. The American Medical Association has compiled many facts and figures available to the writer. He can fairly readily determine and discuss the similarities and differences in training requirements, state examinations, and various types of specializations. He can even determine a general range (that most deceptive of measurements) of possible income for the physician. He can estimate the expense of the training, the time involved, the cost of setting up a practice, and the length of time necessary for the young physician or surgeon to reach the minimum income. The writer encounters even less uniformity when he attempts to describe

---

Only two generalizations seem possible from a thorough review of the works of the authors in the field: (1) those who define the word "work" generally do not define "occupation," and vice versa; and (2) those dealing primarily with occupational information do not define either term.

working conditions and situation, hours of employment, patient and public contact. The specialist in a large city engages in entirely different "work" from that of the general practitioner in a country town. The actual "work" of the radiologist or the researcher, both specialists, may have no resemblance to that of the orthopedic surgeon or the hospital administrator, both of whom are also specialists. The common link of the work is often only the M.D. degree. The penchant of each specialist further enhances the discrepancies. Already, factual description is difficult. The writer's attempt to generalize the information and to make it national in scope further distorts the facts and ruins the authenticity.

The reader of occupational materials reshapes the information presented in terms of his own experiences and learnings. The small-town student or counselor, knowing something of the local physician's charges for calls, working conditions, hours, and contact with patients will interpret what he reads in the light of his own experiences. These experiences and interpretations will be far different from those of the student or counselor in a large city environment.

Because occupational information purports to be national in coverage and relatively brief, it must be general. Generalities beget vagueness. Vagueness in turn engenders stereotypes. Generalized information cannot fulfill the purpose prescribed by methodological theory.

Occupational information can also be misleading. On a national scale there may be a severe shortage of teachers, but in some favored communities there may be an oversupply. Not many occupational brochures point out these regional differences or deal with other important differences in the general shortage picture. There may be an overabundance of English or social studies teachers and a dearth of mathematics and science teachers. There may be plenty of high school teachers and a scarcity of junior high school teachers. There may be severe shortages of personnel in all subjects in some particular school systems, while nearby systems and areas may have an abundance of applicants. Many national generalizations do not apply to particular subjects, levels, and locales.

Analysis reveals many weaknesses in generalized occupational information. These weaknesses raise questions as to whether in a complex civilization one can establish generalizations about occupations. Is it possible to adapt information about occupations for a national reading public without sacrificing the very *raison d'être* of that formal information—its authentic, factual nature?

THE UNKNOWNS. Any formal occupational brochure requires careful research. In order to write authoritatively about salary ranges in any occupation, the author must either collect the statistics himself or rely upon data gathered by other agencies. For some few occupations, various associations, governmental bureaus, and labor unions compile statistics and keep them up to date. For many of the over 40,000 occupations in this country it is impossible to establish a valid salary range because there are no statistics. The writer must become either a researcher or a clairvoyant.

Furthermore, certain "facts" included in occupational pamphlets are not facts at all. Any material treating personal requirements or qualifications is not factual. Practically no research has attempted to discover the personality requirements of specific occupations. At present there are few if any measuring devices that might implement such investigations.

Occupational brochures describing counseling, for example, invariably list the personality traits deemed necessary for a counselor. These usually include such virtues as flexibility, good judgment, understanding, interest in people, emotional stability, personal integrity, and tact. This list is based on assumption only. There is no research to test whether it is valid or invalid, fact or fallacy. Such lists are among the unknowns; in fact there is today absolutely no field for which they are not unknowns.

Another category in the occupational pamphlet in which fiction is more prevalent than fact is usually entitled "Chances for Advancement." "Advancement" is rarely defined. What does it mean? Increased financial return, greater prestige and status, increased responsibility, greater happiness? Essentially, the answer is a function of the individual. The simplest and most popular definition of advancement is increased financial return. Today the channels for such advancement follow a general pattern that entails for most workers a fundamental change in occupation. The worker advances financially through becoming an administrator, a supervisor, or a specialist. The school teacher who wishes to "advance" can do so only through further study leading to greater specialization, or by taking an administrative position. The skilled worker can "advance" by becoming a supervisor or by achieving greater technical skill. In both instances, the work is no longer the same and the worker has, in essence, changed his occupation.

If advancement means changes in the nature of the work a person does, it brings into question the personality characteristics discussed in personal requirements. Are the same personal qualities essential for the generalist, the specialist, and the executive within any given set of occupations? Is the person who enjoys and is good at teaching also the one who will succeed in writing, research, advanced study, specialization, administration, and counseling? There is no research that might clarify the discrepancies between modern routes of advancement and the generalized assumptions about personality constellations in occupations. Until such clarification is accomplished, neither traditional category can be anything but misleading to the reader of "factual" occupational brochures.

Similar ungrounded "facts" appear in almost every category of occupational pamphlets. Some occupations require travel; others do not, but there is no set pattern. The accountant, engineer, or the secretary in some companies may travel more than the proverbial traveling salesman. The fireman may spend more time in an "office" than does the country doctor. Working conditions vary from location to location and from plant to plant. Exceptions are so frequent in all occupations that they preclude generalization.

Research can illuminate some of the unknowns, but until this research is done, much occupational information will remain speciously authentic. The representative of one company producing occupational brochures for sale to schools, for example, assured a prospective client that the information had been carefully prepared. He stated as an illustration that the journalist writing the material on dentistry was especially prepared for his job because his brother was a dentist! Such *expertise* is not likely to produce unbiased, solidly based information about dentistry in general. Much occupational information has only the illusion of authenticity and fact.

CHANGE. The greatest problem in occupational information is that society is not static. Rather, change is the constant. In our modern civilization it is also rapid. Furthermore, it can be subtle and deceptive.

In this era of change, occupational information is perforce out of date. Suppose a writer assembles information about a particular occupation and does a thorough job of it. He gathers material from the statistics and research available to him. The most current figures he can find will be at least a year old, probably older. A report published in 1961 contains figures gathered a year or two before the publication date. The writer then puts together his occupational brochure and waits for publication. By this time, another year or six months has elapsed. Hence on the date of publication, the new occupational pamphlet is about two years old with respect to the information it contains. This lag cannot be prevented and affects any publication.

In most vocational guidance programs, students concentrate on occupational information at the choice points—eighth or ninth grade, when they must choose between academic and vocational curricula, and twelfth grade, when they must seek employment or further education. The junior high school student reads information dealing with the current picture. He does not put that information into use for another four or more years. The senior for whom high school education is terminal will make the most direct use of occupational information. The senior going on to college, however, will not apply the material he reads for another four to ten years.

The occupational information a junior high school vocational student asborbs will be six to eight years out of date by the time he enters the labor force. For the college-bound student, the "facts" he reads in junior high school will be ten to eighteen years out of date by the time he tries to use them! And these figures apply only to information that is the lastest available. Some ambitious school counselors go through their files every few years and weed out the old; many more simply accumulate pamphlets and brochures and may find dates from the 1940's on much of their information. Undated information is worthless, for then the time lag cannot even be estimated.

If society were static, the passé quality of occupational information would not distort the "facts." But increasingly, change is so rapid that the supposedly authentic, factual but out-of-date statements mislead both the counselor and his students.

Obvious changes within the past ten years have been far-reaching on all levels of employment. Space exploration, missile development, electronics, and automation, for example, have produced such drastic changes in the world of work that new occupations have developed and old ones have been completely altered or eliminated. Almost any decade during the first half of the twentieth century presents a picture of similar changes. Mass production of the automobile effected changes in industry, mobility, culture, and mores and created new occupations now taken for granted—occupations ranging from gas station attendant to highway engineer to specialized mechanic to smog expert. No one knows what the next ten years will produce. At the beginning of the 1950's few people would have predicted space probes, and counselors would have labeled the idea of them "fantasy."

Subtle change is much more deceptive. Many occupations have borne the same name for decades, even centuries. These ame-name occupations are usually the most familiar: physician, teacher, bookkeeper, conductor, engineer, lawyer, and many more. More often than not, the old names confer on the occupation an illusion of sameness that distorts perspective. The actual nature of the work done by a modern physician or engineer may have no similarity to that done by his predecessor. The link is literally through name only.

Such subtle change often misleads both the counselor and his students. The counselor views the world from his background of experience and age and the student from his. The counselor often administers interest inventories developed on occupational groups studied in the 1930's and 1940's (people who received their training in the 1910's or 1920's) and uses his findings with students who will seek employment in the 1960's or 1970's. The counselor encourages students to read the "facts" about occupations in terms of what they *were,* not what they *are* or *will become.* Similarity in occupational names has led everyone astray.

Usually information deals with specific occupations. Perhaps the concentration on specifics has dulled the importance of change. Obvious and subtle changes are constant in our society, and occupational information perforce ignores them. Since it does, it cannot be either authentic or factual.

MOTIVATION. The student's chief sources of formal educational information are occupational brochures and college catalogues. The latter contain many facts and most of them are revised every year, hence they do not share many of the shortcomings inherent in occupational information. They do, however, share some of the motivational weaknesses.

Most formal information follows a traditional structure developed at least half a century ago. The contents of occupational pamphlets are determined and limited by the familiar Parsonian structure. College catalogues follow a pattern of entrance requirements, course offerings, and minimum requirements for a major and a degree, plus brief information about scholarships, housing, grading system, and the history of the college. Faculty names and degrees may or may not be included. Both of these sources of information are written in a formal, sometimes unreadable, style. Some colleges supplement their catalogues with less imposing publications dealing with campus life. In general, however, tradition dictates both the contents and the style of formal information.[3]

The traditional structures were outlined before motivational theories came into being. To date, the format has not been altered to take into account the little that is known about motivation. This lack of change means that all formal publications have serious omissions. Where can the student find the information that is most important to him? "Facts" about the prestige and status of various occupations or colleges? About how well or ill an occupation or a college coincides with his picture of it? All the additional information that essentially deals with what he as a person is seeking from employment or education?

The answer is simple. The student searches informal sources for the knowledge that is most essential to him. He finds out about colleges and jobs from all the informal sources that have meaning for him. On the basis of what his friends are doing, what his parents want him to do, what his school experiences and learnings have been, what he sees around him, what is important to him, and myriad other influences he makes his decisions. He decides to go on to higher education or not, to take a particular job or not.

Whether formal information is authentic or factual is a minor problem in comparison with its major weakness. It simply does not touch upon the materials most important to the youngster facing decisions. All formal information is compiled and written *by* adults *for* adults and covers the topics adults think student

[3] The college catalogue is, in one sense, a legal document and must therefore, be written in language that covers all contingencies. Printing a catalogue is expensive, so that one publication must present all information. Writers on occupations do not have these excuses. From the point of view of the students, all formal information is deadly dull.

should find meaningful. Adults expect students to make decisions in a way that adults themselves never employ.

Basically the whole problem goes back to outmoded concepts of how students learn and make decisions. Regardless of wishful thinking and unrealistic theorizing, a vocational or educational decision is not an intellectual reasoning about two sets of questionable facts. The "facts" are unimportant unless they are dramatic and in conflict with the self-concept and firmly held values of the individual. The student makes decisions the way everyone makes them—out of the totality of his being.

The Myths

The informational area has been founded on several *assumptions:* (1) that formal information is authentic and factual; (2) that specific information about the world of work is valid for and applicable to the future; (3) that such information meets student needs and produces important learnings; and (4) that such information furnishes the basis for reasoned decisions. Tradition and usage have made these false assumptions seemingly inviolate; they are the informational myths.

These myths furnish the basis for much of vocational guidance practice. The wide acceptance of them can be seen in the fact that more government funds have gone into the production of occupational information than into any other area of guidance and counseling. More school time and money are devoted to classes in occupations and the purchase of "factual" information than to any other aspect of the school counseling program. Much money and time have been wasted preserving the myths.

The informational myths have had another important subtle influence. They have helped to create the modern myth of realism.

Chapter 5

REALISM

ONE OF THE words bandied about most frequently in the literature of vocational counseling is realism. The student must make
a realistic appraisal of his personal assets and liabilities. He must
study realistically information about various occupations and
possible careers open to him. Then, on the basis of these two
"realities," he must make a realistic decision about his future.
The assumption, of course, is that three "realities" are better
than one.

And yet nowhere in the literature can one find a definition
or discussion of realism. Perhaps it is impossible to define or
discuss a term which in and of itself represents the ultimate in
the definite. Nevertheless, some discussion of the concept of
realism is necessary because of its growing popularity as a basic
premise in vocational counseling. Each counselor needs to know
what he means by realism and the realistic self-concept and how
these meanings are expressed in his work with students. Such exploration will justify the inclusion of realism under the heading
of the myths of vocational and occupational counseling.

The Meaning of Realism

The word realism is essentially a mask for a value judgment
about the practicality and the practicability of an idea, a feeling,
or a plan. Such a judgment is made at a certain point in time

and on the basis of a particular set of circumstances. Suppose that ten years ago an able student with marked scientific interests had said to his counselor, "I want to be a space explorer and I'm going to make that my career." At that time his counselor would undoubtedly have labeled this career plan unrealistic. Today his counselor would applaud the plan because in the fullness of time it has acquired elements of the practical and the practicable.

The person who looks at the world realistically is rather like the horse wearing blinders: he sees what is before him on the race track, but he cannot look to either side and, because his vision is so channeled, he can look up only with difficulty. Realism precludes the vision that looks out, above, and beyond to what is not there, as well as to what is. Was the student unrealistic when he thought of space exploration ten years ago? The scientific theories were ready, rockets were then beyond the experimental stage, and some men had plans for space probes. Or was the student, untrammeled by the need to be realistic, able to exercise vision?

Dr. Thomas Dooley was called unrealistic when he conceived the idea of MEDICO and its hospital outposts in Laos and other underdeveloped countries. But his idea worked and it won support throughout the world after its practicability had been proved. From the point of view of people unwilling to work for an idea and to accept the disappointments and frustrations that are inevitable in implementing it, Dooley was unrealistic. From his own point of view, however, Dooley wanted to do something and he did it. Nothing for him could have been more realistic.

Realism is a judgment dependent upon time and the point of view of the person making it. Through usage the word has taken on moral connotations—realism is "good" and lack of realism is "bad." These connotations endow the adjectives realistic and unrealistic with strong value qualities. Even the counselor who would never say, "That would be a bad occupation for you" does not hesitate to label the student's choice unrealistic. To the student, the meaning is the same. Realism is good and

unrealism is bad; realism is worthy, suitable, sensible, and leads
to approval, while unrealism is hare-brained, ill-conceived, un-
thinking, and leads to lectures on the importance of growing up.
Values are inseparable from judgments about realism.

In the schools the counselor is the person who assesses the
quantity of realism of a student's educational and vocational
plans. The counselor's values are inextricably bound up in his
estimates of realism and these estimates accrue from his background. The counselor sees vocational plans from his own point
of view and labels them accordingly. His own needs affect this
process of labeling plans realistic or unrealistic. The counselor
who needs prestige and status will view askance a student's
choice of an occupation lacking these. The counselor who values
monetary returns might question a student's decision to become
a clergyman, because the financial rewards will be limited. The
counselor who wants security would label the student's plan to
become an actor unrealistic because of the difficulties and the
uncertainty of success. The counselor to whom masculinity per
se is of major importance will express his feelings about a boy's
desire to become a poet or a ballet dancer through the polite
label "unrealistic." The counselor having strong objections to
careers for women may discourage a girl's desire to seek pro-
tracted training by emphasizing marriage and homemaking as
the necessary realisms in her plan. Perhaps nowhere in counseling are the needs and values of the counselor more evident
than in his discussions with students about their vocational
plans. In these discussions his values predominate.

Just as a counselor's personal values and needs are reflected in
his use of the words realistic and unrealistic, so are his cultural
values. Certainly in the days when the strip-tease dancer was
still a member of the social scene, counselors did not regard this
activity as an appropriate career choice for girls. And yet for
some girls, might it not have been a realistic choice and one
which could open the way to material success and perhaps some
fame? Today the gambling tables in Las Vegas need dealers
and there is even a school which trains dealers. The work i

not hard, the hours are short, the pay is excellent, and the working environment is luxurious. Dealing might be a realistic occupational choice for the youngster who likes cards, dice, and probabilities. But would any counselor suggest it? Counselors often sacrifice "realism" for the "greater good" of moralism.

More often than not, the student is considered realistic if and when he agrees with the counselor's appraisal of his plans and decisions. Counselors view realism in terms not of the student, but of their own knowledge, experience, background, needs, and values. Realism has become such a popular goal that its influence has pervaded all of education. The concept of realism as an aim in the development of the whole individual is detrimental.

The Realistic Self-Concept

An individual's self-concept includes three things: the person's own intimate view of himself or his ego; his perception of how others view him or his idea of his social self; and his idea of the person he would like to be or his ideal self. These three phases of the self-concept coalesce to form an individual's total picture of himself—a picture that influences the person in all his actions, thoughts, and feelings. The self-concept is composed not only of private inner thoughts, feelings, attitudes, and values, but also of experiences, expectations, attitudes, values, and opinions derived from other people and their cultures.

The self-concept grows, develops, and changes throughout the life of the individual. An infant begins to learn to view himself in certain ways because of the treatment accorded him. If he is handled gently and tenderly and his physical needs are satisfied without undue delay, he acquires some sense of himself as a worth-while human being. As the child grows older, he learns what he can and cannot do both through experience and through the attitudes of adults, siblings, and peers. He also begins to develop his concept of an ideal self through his learnings and his identification with various adults. Particularly in adolescence, the youngster goes through a period of upheaval as his concept of self loses many of its childish "unrealistic" aspects and begins to incorporate the image of himself as an adult. This change makes the adolescent especially vulnerable to the realistic judgments of adults. Although the greatest changes may take place during adolescence, the self-concept is never static but continues to modify throughout the adult years. New experiences, new interpersonal relationships, and new learnings make of the self-concept a malleable core of personality.

Self-concept is based upon a person's perceptions and what he internalizes from what he perceives. It is well-known that no two people perceive precisely the same things in the same way with the same interpretations and meanings. Unfortunately, investigations into perception and its subjective elements are so embryonic that no theories that might broaden the knowledge of self-concept exist.

There are, however, two generalizations that the counselor stressing realism should keep in mind. First, telling the student that his views are unrealistic does not change those views. The teen-ager who has never known success or who has learned to view himself as less able than his brothers or sisters cannot suddenly view himself as able simply because the counselor tells him he is. The girl who has learned to view herself as unattractive cannot be talked into another self-concept. Many people judged by others to be able or beautiful do not see themselves in terms of these "realities," which are essentially comparisons and value judgments.

The second point that the counselor should consider is that his derogatory statements made in the cause of realism are most likely to be internalized because they reinforce the feelings of inferiority the student is apt to have. The counselor who remarks, "I don't think you're college material"; or "Are you sure your idea of going to college is realistic?" may wish to shield the student from failure. The student hears the value judgment and reacts to it by agreement or strong disagreement. Either way the judgments reinforce inferiorities.

Perhaps "realism" serves most completely as a delimiting device in terms of the student's concept of his ideal self. Apparently the ideal of self must also be realistic—an obvious contradiction in terms. The ideal self provides a model toward which the individual strives and sets the standards for his evaluation of himself. Certainly for some individuals this ideal is so unattainable that they find themselves experiencing constant anxiety about their failures to progress toward it, and for these persons some modification of the ideal in the direction of realism is desirable. But the realism has to be theirs, not the counselor's.

All too often counselors see their role as that of modifying the ideal toward greater realism as they, not the students, envision realism. Many students tend to downgrade themselves—to view themselves as less than they actually are. Counselors striving to help these students have tended to work toward greater "realism" of the ideal rather than a more "realistic" assessment of the self. Counseling that might help the student to understand his own views of self and to have successful experiences is bypassed in favor of lowering the ideal toward greater conformity with the view of self. What counselors often call realism might more aptly be called downgrading.

Many gifted youngsters tend to undervalue themselves. These students are the ones who are most susceptible to the counselor's stress on realism, for it reinforces their doubts. They are also most sensitive to the cultural emphasis on practicability and the setting of "realistic" goals. This combination of pressures often forces the gifted student to lower his already downgraded goals. For him, the stress upon realism is a disservice of the most insidious kind.

Before any counselor may with justification base his work upon the idea of the realistic self-concept, he must ask himself a number of questions. Realism for what purpose? Realism from whose point of view? Realism on the basis of what data?

In any counseling, guidance, or advisory relationship, there are a number of realities involved—those of the counselor, those of the student, and a third that might be called the "true reality." This third reality is like sigma, the true standard deviation for a total population, which can be only approximated even with the use of the most refined statistical procedures. This is so because true reality is colored by the attitudes, biases, perceptions, values, and idiosyncratic views of the individuals involved. Who, then, is to say what is realistic or when a student has a realistic self-concept?

Realism and Facts

The counselor's realism is a value judgment based upon the collection of "facts" in his files about a particular student. He has such specific information as home address, family members, citizenship, age, and place of birth which might properly be labeled factual. He has the student's academic record which, especially if the grades are stated numerically, may give a reassuring appearance of being factual. Actually, these grades are a set of many teachers' value judgments about the student and his performance in various subject-matter areas. Hence grades are less factual than age or home address. The counselor also has the student's test scores in his record folder. A review of Chapter II will remind the reader of the many fallacies of test scores. With IQ scores liable to be misleading, interest rankings not really testing interests, aptitude scores highly contaminated by achievement, and personality scores worthless, test scores cannot be considered as facts, but only as suggestive samples of the student's behavior at a particular point in time. In addition, the counselor may have teachers' comments about the student, but these are by no means facts. They are only opinions and value judgments based upon experiences with the student at a particular time in his life. Essentially, most of the "facts" in the counselor's possession are not facts at all, but only bits of information highly contaminated by limitations, personal biases, feelings, and thoughts. And yet it is on these "facts" that many "realistic" decisions are based.

A counselor has one other source of "facts"—interviews with the student himself. Here again the question inevitably arises,

Is what the student says about himself factual? Depending upon his relationship with the counselor, a student may supply considerable information regarding himself, his thoughts, feelings, interests, and aspirations. Some of this information will present an accurate picture from the student's point of view of how he feels and thinks at the moment. The student would say he is being factual, and he is, insofar as he can know and express the facts. Nevertheless, what he says is colored by his self-protective defenses, his desire to please the counselor, his inability to view himself objectively, and his uncertainty about himself and what he wants to do or can do. Perhaps what the student says about himself is the most meaningful set of "facts" the counselor has. But what the student says may not be factual from any point of view except his own.

The data available to the counselor form the basis upon which he and the student arrive at realistic decisions and plans for the student's future. But how can these decisions and plans be realistic when they are based upon facts that are not facts? Certainly the counselor must use any and all data that might contribute to his greater understanding of the student, but he should not fool himself into believing that the data are static facts or that the decisions based upon such data are necessarily realistic.

Counselors sometimes forget who is making the decision and from whose point of view the realism has to be judged. Suppose a student with a high IQ and good grades in science decides to be an actor despite all he has heard and read about the difficulties in achieving success in that career. Who is to say the decision is unrealistic? From the counselor's point of view it may seem impractical, chancy, and slightly unpatriotic. From the student's point of view, however, this career may be the only practical, realistic one for him in terms of his perceptions, interests, feelings, and desires.

Some of the emphasis upon realism stems from the counselor's fear that the student will fail. And he may. But then he may fail in anything he undertakes. The danger of failure lurks in any activity, but people have not allowed this to immobilize them and probably never will. Failure can be an extremely constructive experience for the individual if he learns from it and can go on to new experiences where he can apply his added understanding. Every person has the right to try—and the right to fail. Fear of failure is not an adequate base for forcing a "realistic" decision about careers.

In part the stress upon the realistic vocational decision grows out of the idea that a student will make a single vocational choice. There is no such thing as a single vocational choice, but rather a series of them extending over a lifetime. Even the student who knows surely and early that he wants to go into a specific vocation still faces myriad occupational decisions. The student whose ideas about what he wants to do are less definite may make many vocational decisions before he finishes his career. In these circumstances an emphasis upon "realism" is more likely to narrow a student's perspectives than to help him broaden his occupational understandings.

Realism as it operates in vocational counseling is delimiting. All occupational and vocational guidance is directed toward helping the student to make a vocational choice, which of course means that the student has to eliminate job areas as he progresses toward a decision. This process of elimination is in its very nature limiting. Moreover, the student can develop some knowledge of only a few of the over 40,000 kinds of work in this country, usually those within his own experience or that of his parents and other adults, or those to which he is introduced in his school. Necessarily, the latter are limited by the penchant and experience of the person teaching about occupations. Hence the student is again limited in his opportunities for acquaintance with and exploration of work areas. And yet counselors want him to make a realistic choice, while their methods of delimiting the student are about as unrealistic as possible! When possible job areas are many and varied and constantly expanding, a point of view and a process which narrow and delimit a student early in his development by whatever means and for whatever purpose represent the height of un-realism.

Some of the misunderstandings and misinterpretations of realism grow out of the original conception of vocational guidance and the static qualities of its theories. The basic premises of vocational guidance were formulated in terms of a limited atypical group before any of the major developments in psychology, sociology, and anthropology were achieved, before work in the United States had attained its highly technological character, and before the high school diploma had become virtually a universal acquisition. The concept of realism has, like the rest of vocational guidance, failed to grow with the years. Counselors have not recognized that realism is relative to the person, the situation, and the counselor. They have failed to take into account the discrepancy between the realism which characterizes the vocational decision of the average student of moderate ability and that which typifies the vocational aspirations of the highly gifted student. They have ignored the realism which is relative to the community and its geographical location in favor of a realism that smacks of the national and para-doxically operates from a completely provincial base. Perhaps the most serious misunderstanding of realism arises from the counselor's belief that he is helping the student to be realistic, when actually he is merely imposing his personal value of realism upon the student.

Realism and the Realities

One of the criteria by which one can judge mental health and stability is the contact with reality displayed by the individual. This contact means that the individual has some understanding of what is going on around him, can communicate with other people, and understands those other people to some extent. When counselors speak of a student understanding the realities of a situation, however, their judgment is likely to be based upon far more mundane considerations. The student who understands the realities is likely to be the one who recognizes a good salary, generous fringe benefits, ample retirement plan, and all the rest, and, on the counselor's advice, makes the "right" vocational decision. The student who accepts the counselor's judgments knows the realities.

Naturally there are some realities which everyone must accept. The reality of the law and its prohibitions against robbery, assault, and murder is one that students and counselors alike must recognize and take into account in their planning. For most students, this acceptance of legal realities is not too difficult because the law is for them merely a formalized expression of some of their own cultural values. Other realities, however, are neither so closely related to values nor so likely to produce immediate and direct retribution. The counselor thinks of the realities in terms of the things that are most important and necessary to him, and so does the teen-ager. And one set of realities is no less realistic than the other when both are viewed in terms of the developmental stages of the counselor and the student, and the progress each has made toward that elusive goal, maturity.

Essentially the enforcement of realism on students is simply another weapon in the long battle to produce conforming adults out of non-conforming children. Conformity to the laws and to some parts of the social codes is highly desirable in a society of over 180 million people, for it allows those people to live together in some degree of harmony. But need the young always conform to the ideas of the old? Must youngsters be limited by the myth of realism? Must teen-agers accept their counselors' definitions of the realities? According to the counselors they should, but luckily many teen-agers do not. The nation is fortunate that young people choose to ignore the stress on realism, for if they did not there would be few writers, inventors, experimental scientists—few people, in fact, in any of the fields of endeavor that require the student to gamble unrealistically on his own abilities and potentialities.

Part II

ACTUALITIES

These, then, are the myths that have dubiously served the vocational counselor. Tied as they are to a world that no longer exists, to a theory antique and unsupportable, and to methods superficially objective, factual, and simple but fundamentally unsound, the myths have survived because they offer pseudo-scientific short cuts and support entrenched interest.

In the modern world, however, myths are dangerous allies. No amount of wishful thinking, reminiscing, blind faith, or political maneuvering can bring back past time or conditions. Modern man may rue the passing of the horse or the Model T as means of transportation, but he boards a jet airliner for his hurried business trip across the continent or his pleasure trip to a European capital. En route, he may read about plans for interplanetary travel. He has to live in the modern world and look to the future. During the next two decades, vocational counselors must visualize the present and future worlds of work, not the past; what is and may be, not what was. Survival itself may depend on a forward not a backward look.

Unfortunately, people find comfort in certainty. Man knows, or feels he knows, what happened yesterday. The counselor with statistics and profile sheets at his finger tips feels better able to help the student, for only with such appurtenances can he be that overrated citizen of the modern world, the expert. Somehow *expertise* becomes confused with knowledge of facts and the ability to talk knowingly about them. An expert is certain. But the world of work that lies ahead contains few certainties. Perhaps the only ones are that the next two decades will be years of vast changes reaching into all areas of life and that the student of today will live in a world far different from the present. These two certainties can be either challenging or disquieting. Rarely are they comforting.

What, then, are the actualities of the future? They are the results of trends now in evidence. The actualities include bigness and growth in many areas; modern phenomena that are rapidly becoming an integral part of the work scene; special problems relating to work that have their roots in recent developments; and values pertaining to work that are at an enigmatic midway point between the traditional and the new.

Today, change is actual and rapid. The world which parents and counselors grew up in is not the world of today, and certainly not the world of tomorrow. Communication between people of different generations is more difficult today than ever before. The counselor wishing to communicate with the modern student cannot do so with reference to a world other than that of the student, a world of change, trends, and resultant actualities. If the counselor does not look to the future he will lose contact with the student, and without communication there is no counseling. Guidance and counseling cannot rest on myths; they have to be built on actualities.

Chapter 6

CHANGES IN SIZE

THE FIRST of the actualities is a continuing trend toward bigness in population, cities, business and industry, and educational institutions. This trend, present since the country began to expand, has taken on new dimensions within the past twenty-five years. Only during the past decade, however, has bigness become a fact of life to many people.

There are literally more people everywhere. The person who sought solitude a decade ago in an area outside a large city now finds himself surrounded by other exurbanites. As he drives to work he competes with more automobiles. If he travels on trains, subways, or buses, he is jostled and crowded by more people on the public transportation. He and his wife join fifty thousand people to see a ball game and a million people to swim at a public beach. Their children may go to school only half of each school day in classes of fifty or sixty, or to new schools enrolling twice as many students as the old and becoming overcrowded at once. Bigness is evident in all facets of existence.

The final reports from the 1960 census are already obsolete. At no time can one say there are exactly so many people in the United States or in any community, for the figures change every second as new births and deaths are recorded. The best figures are estimates at a given time at a given place, incorporating all the familiar errors. Whereas estimates are available, certainties are not. One can be sure only of the trend.

Nevertheless, the counselor has more objective evidence about changes in size than about other changes. He can look about him and see the trend toward bigness and anticipate many of the effects that such increases will have.

Trends toward Bigness

Already increases in size pose problems for the nation. These present problems, however, are insignificant compared to what will happen within the next two decades. The trend toward bigness is well established. Perhaps the expected growth in population, cities, business and industry, and education are the most important for the counselor's knowledge of the future.

POPULATION.   According to the 1960 United States Census reports, the population of the country is now over 180,000,000. In 1950 the Census reported over 150,000,000. This growth in population during the 1950's is roughly equivalent to the total population of the country a century ago. The table on the opposite page indicates the magnitude of the growth. The growth in population since 1900 almost equals the total population of the nation in 1920.[1]

Spectacular as has been the growth since the turn of the century, it will be far overshadowed by the increases to come. Even the most cautious prognosticators estimate that the population will reach 260 million by 1980. Bigness breeds bigger bigness.

[1] Census figures are never exactly comparable from decade to decade. The 1960 census, for example, includes the new states of Hawaii and Alaska. Such adulteration, however, does not fundamentally change the amazing picture of growth. The 1960 population of the United States is 179,323,175 according to the final count. This figure does not include members of Armed Services and their dependents overseas, people on ships, and people residing overseas. When these figures are in, the population total will reach over 180,000,000. Hence the 1960 total is indicated in the table as 180+ million. The rounded-off figures are much more useful and significant than the actual figures for the counselor, who must remember that census figures are at best estimates.

Year	Rounded-Off Census Figures (in Millions)
1790	3.9
1800	5.3
1810	7.2
1820	9.6
1830	12.9
1840	17.1
1850	23.2
1860	31.4
1870	38.6
1880	50.2
1890	62.9
1900	76.0
1910	92.0
1920	105.7
1930	122.8
1940	131.7
1950	150.7
1960	180+

Of greater significance to the counselor than sheer numbers are the age groupings of the population and the implications of these groupings for his counseling. The first important change is well-known: people live longer today than they ever lived before. The early vocational counselors knew that a white male child born in 1910 could be expected to live for about forty-nine years. The white male child born today will probably live to be seventy or older, until A.D. 2030 or beyond. Medical research is steadily increasing longevity and will continue to do so through growing knowledge of the degenerative diseases, especially cancer and cardiovascular ailments. Currently, one out of every eleven people is sixty-five or older. The youngsters with whom vocational counselors work will not die on the job, but will live past retirement and well into the twenty-first century.

There will be increasing numbers of people not only in the over sixty-five age group but also in the the under twenty group. This second change has presented acute problems during the past decade and these problems will increase during the coming years. If the birth rate remains constant or even declines, the number of people under twenty will continue to increase because the base population is larger. Then, too, people are getting married younger, fewer mothers are dying in childbirth, and infant mortality has decreased. Whereas a century ago only one-fourth of the infants born survived until age five, today one-fourth of those born may live eighty-three years, and one-half of them almost seventy-four years. By 1980 approximately 42 per cent of the population of the United States will be in the under twenty age group, and about 50 per cent will be under twenty-five.

While the nonproductive age groups in the population will increase, the most productive will be relatively small. The effects of the severe depression are reflected in the lowered birth rate during the 1930's. The people born in 1930 make up the group that will be forty in 1970 and those born in 1940 will be forty in 1980. Despite small changes due to limited immigration, one of the certain facts about the population is the maximum size of the group that will reach the middle years during the next two decades—these people have already been born. The lowered birth rate during the depression years means that proportionately fewer people than might have been expected will be the productive core of the population in 1970 and 1980.

What do these figures about the age groups of the population mean? In general within our occupational structure, the people under twenty or over sixty-five are consumers of goods and services, not producers. As these two groups increase, a proportionately smaller group of people will have to produce the goods and services for the entire population. The most productive group will be the smallest—those born during the depression years. Of the population in the productive age group, slightly more than half are women. Unless all the women work, the productive group becomes even smaller in comparison with the total population. Furthermore, only a small percentage of this group has had sufficient education to enable its members to keep up with developments in an increasingly technological world.

The effects of the population explosion and the changing composition of that population are all part of the current trend toward bigness. Barring pestilence, plague, famine, and hydrogen bombs, these population trends will not change significantly. The school counselor needs to keep them in mind. The youngster he counsels today will live in the world created by the trends that are only now becoming evident.

URBANIZATION. When, in 1892, Frederick Jackson Turner postulated 1890 as the closing of the frontier, there were a little over twenty-one people for every square mile in this country. Now there are about sixty. In 1890 over 40 per cent of the labor force worked in agriculture; today less than 10 per cent are so employed. In 1890 farms averaged about 135 acres in size; today they average over 300 acres. Where, then, do over 180 million people live and work? Ever increasingly, around and in the large cities.

The move to the cities has been evident since the country began to grow, but in no decade has it been so striking as in the 1950's. About 85 per cent of the total population increase occurred in cities of 50,000 or more and in the suburbs surrounding them.

Even a brief glance at the Census figures for 1960 and 1950 illuminates the nature of the move toward the cities. In general, while the population of the city itself may have dropped slightly, that of the metropolitan area has increased dramatically. New York City and Minneapolis, Minnesota, provide excellent examples of this trend. Manhattan, the heart of New York City, has decreased in population as old residences have been demolished and replaced by office buildings. Although more people work in the limited space of Manhattan, fewer people live there. The area around Manhattan, however, presents a picture of startling growth. Levittown, a semi-rural area in 1950, now claims a population of over 65,000 people; Hicksville now has over 50,000 residents.

In much the same manner, the city of Minneapolis declined in population, but such new suburbs as Bloomington mushroomed from an unincorporated village to a city of over 50,000. Occasionally the picture of suburban growth is reflected in the population of the city itself because the boundaries of the metropolitan area have been extended.

Urban areas have multiplied in certain geographical regions. The sudden inflation of population in the southwest and western areas is duplicated only in Alaska and Florida. The total population of Nevada increased by over 78 per cent, with the four major cities doubling, tripling, or quadrupling in size. Arizona's population increased almost 74 per cent, with Tuscon expanding from 45,000 to almost 213,000 people. California made the largest net gain—over 5,000,000 people, comprising roughly one-fifth of the population increase of the United States—although its percentage of increase was 48.5 per cent. Americans have certainly heeded Horace Greeley's advice, "Go west, young man," and even limited it to "Go to the western cities."

Whereas most metropolitan areas have grown, small cities have sprung into the 100,000 population category, and new cities of 25,000 or more have come into being, the picture is not the same throughout the entire country. The percentage gain in population for the northeastern states was only one-third that of the western states. Many cities of the 5,000 to 15,000 size in predominantly agricultural areas remained the same or actually declined. Many cities of all sizes dependent largely upon a single industry reflected in population the decline or growth of that industry. For example, despite the emergence of taconite processing and the opening of the St. Lawrence Seaway, the population of the iron-range cities of Minnesota and their port city, Duluth, has remained relatively stable. At a time when the total population is increasing rapidly, lack of or only slight growth is equivalent to decline.

What does this trend toward the cities imply? Twenty years from now, the eastern and western seaboards will be one continuous line of cities marked off only by city limits and the land reserved for parks and game sanctuaries. Increasingly, too, there will be fewer of the latter as land becomes more valuable and the game seemingly less so. Already the trend can be seen on the east coast between New York City and Washington; in a different way, in the series of cabanas, motels, and hotels rapidly lining the Florida coasts; and on the west coast in the intermingled resorts, oil wells, and factories along the California coastline.

The largest cities of the future will probably not be the present well-known ones. Population growth is like a geometric progression and, if present trends continue, the largest cities in the United States may be in the southwest and the west, not on the eastern seaboard or in the meat-packing, railroad centers of the middle west.

More people will be living and working closer together and traveling greater distances from their homes to their work. The worker seeking a modern-day version of Walden Pond will not find it. While Thoreau felt civilization encroaching on his domain, his modern prototype will find suburbs literally surrounding his.

BUSINESSES AND INDUSTRIES. Today's counselor needs no Census or business reports to depict the industrial changes occurring around him. He needs only to view his own community and to acknowledge the changes he fears, welcomes, or ignores. The trends toward bigness in industries and businesses are evident from the point of view of both the consumer and the producer.

Today, in most communities, a consumer drives his car (the product of mass production) to the nearest shopping center, a modern-day phenomenon located outside the center of the community, where huge parking lots are possible. He pushes a self-service cart through block-long stores to pick up his groceries, drugs, hardware, and other small products. His own large refrigerator and freezer allow him to stock frozen foods which make cooking a matter of reading instructions and setting an oven. The modern supermarket, although in many ways a return to the old general trading post, differs widely from its progenitor. It is impersonal, part of a chain of similar markets, and an ever-present symbol of big business.

The old specialties of small tradesmen no longer exist. The huge drug store sells hardware, small furniture, sporting goods, cosmetics, candies, and appliances and so does the supermarket. Hardware stores being squeezed on small items must turn to larger items for their profits. The small speciality shop, unless it is located in a large city and deals in luxury articles for the "carriage trade," has a precarious existence. The shopper no longer needs the separate meat market, for example, because he buys his meats, fresh or already cooked, in the supermarket. More often than not, his present-day desires in meats are limited—steaks, chops, chicken pieces, an occasional roast, and ready-cooked items. Competition and the shopper's consciousness of time and diet have written finis to the old-time meat market.

Increasingly, the stores through which the shopper pushes his cart are not locally owned or operated or even managed. But many individual shoppers own stock in the company or in some mutual fund investing his money in stocks.

Today's consumer buys large items on a credit plan—so much down and so much to pay each week or month. This buying plan is possible because of the large capital of the big retailers. Installment buying has placed within many homes products that even ten years ago were not dreamed attainable. The scales used a decade or so ago by sociologists to determine the socioeconomic standing of a family are not applicable today. The questions asked usually concerned the possession of a sofa, telephone, automobile, radio, indoor plumbing, newspapers, and magazines —and in the more recent lists, a television set. Today well over 85 per cent of the population has a TV set, and the other 15 per cent includes many who could afford one but prefer other recreation. A frequent complaint among the unemployed is that they are bored with watching television.

Credit buying has not only boosted store sales, but also made money lending a vast enterprise. Banks have expanded their credit departments and finance companies have become popular everywhere. In 1960 American consumers ran up a bill of more than 56 billion dollars—a 4 billion dollar increase over the record in 1959. The have-it-now, pay-later, and trade-it-in craze has created the sharp rise in the standard of living for most Americans. One can sit on the partially owned chair in the partially owned dwelling, cook on the partially owned stove, watch the partially owned television, listen to the partially owned stereophonic set, and even travel around the world on a partially owned ticket. Some housewives in California are currently trying to organize a Charge Accounts Anonymous to perform the same function for credit enthusiasts that Alcoholics Anonymous offers its members.

From the producer's point of view many subtle and direct changes have occurred. The first of these concerns the conduct of research. Robert Fulton built his own steamboat and tried it out himself. Henry Ford assembled his first automobile in his own garage. Some new products are still developed in this fashion, but only rarely. Research is now an integral part of big business and industry. Research is no longer an individual enterprise; rather it is a team operation that is as much the province of big business as are production lines.

The old-time picture of big business has changed. Bigness today is far different from that in the early 1900's when Teddy Roosevelt campaigned for anti-trust legislation to break the monopolistic practices of the robber barons. Today's large companies are not individually or family owned, but controlled by stockholders. No single industrial concern completely controls one field of operation. Large companies offer contracts to a variety of smaller specialized companies. Competition arises not only from large domestically owned concerns but also from foreign enterprises. Competition as well as ownership is international.

With these fundamental changes in bigness there is also greater stress on a "scientific" approach. Managers and executives are trained people with college degrees in business and management; markets are analyzed and production is studied scientifically. Figures on productivity per man-hour of work have gone up steadily as machines have been improved and more skillful technicians have been employed to deal with them. Even labor unions are big business, incorporating as many specialties and as much of a scientific approach as business itself.

Because the new nature of big business and industry demands trained employees, large companies have entered education as never before. Subsidies of employees' education, training programs within the company, sponsorship of research on college campuses, support of scholarships, grants to educational institutions to try out new methods or to raise teachers' salaries are all commonplace. All are an outgrowth of bigness and its needs. Perhaps the most fundamental result of bigness is that the worker of tomorrow will have to be highly educated and trained.

EDUCATION.   Except for slight, temporary drops reflecting the lowered birth rate during the depression years, public school enrollment has risen steadily. The enrollment of 15.5 million students in 1900 has increased to over 35 million in 1960 and is anticipated to be 42.5 million by 1970 and 70 million by 1980. During the last few years, school enrollments have risen over a million students per year, and this trend will continue at a higher rate during the next two decades. By 1970 the 42.5 million students will include 32 million in elementary school, a 15 per cent increase, and 12.4 million in high school, a 47.5 per cent increase.[2]

Rapid growth will also occur in the number of students in private schools and institutions of higher education. In fact, private school enrollment has increased proportionately faster than public school. In 1950 enrollment in nonpublic schools was a little under 12 per cent of that in public schools. Cur-

---

[2] Education statistics are available in the Census reports, the United States Office of Education surveys, and the research bulletins of the National Education Association.

rently this figure is over 16 per cent and is continuing to rise. During the 1950's institutions of higher education felt intensely the growing demand for extended education. College enrollment passed the million mark in 1930 and the 3.5 million mark in 1960. By 1970 there will probably be 7 million college students, about 44 per cent of all individuals eighteen to twenty-one years of age in the country.

With more people obtaining more education, the educational level of the population has risen steadily. In 1940 the median number of years of school completed was 8.6 for men and 8.7 for women. This median passed 9.0 for both groups in 1950, and 10.0 in 1957. By 1980 the median level of education is expected to be 12.2 years, meaning that one-half the population will have had 12 or more years of school. Less than 5 per cent of the total population had completed college in 1940, roughly 8 per cent in 1960, and by 1980 this figure is expected to be over 10 per cent. These figures mean that the younger members of the population will have spent more time on formal education.

However, levels of educational attainment can be deceptive. Although by 1980 almost 3 out of every 5 adults will have completed high school, 2 out of 5 will not have done so. In 1950 a total of 5.5 million children between five and seventeen years of age were not enrolled in any school. Dropout rates in both high schools and colleges remain high. College *graduates* totaled less than 400,000 in 1950 and have yet to reach the half-million mark in any given year.

Furthermore, educational attainment varies widely from one section of the country to another and from one group to another. Of those men from eighteen to twenty-six years of age who failed the Armed Forces Qualification Test during the first year of the Korean War, the greatest number came from the Southern states. The range included 1.3 per cent failures in Minnesota to 56.0 failures in South Carolina, with eight states recording a failure rate higher than 30 per cent. Of those registering for the services at the time of the Korean War, 11 per cent had had less than five years of schooling. In general, the median level of education is higher for white people than for Negroes, and for women than for men.

Educational enrollments will create many problems within the next two decades. First, educational facilities will lag behind enrollments, thereby necessitating expanded building programs. The tax strain will be hardest on the suburban communities. As more people move to the suburbs, more children will go to school there. In fact, over three-fourths of the total anticipated increase in school enrollments will take place in the suburban communities. The new schools built in the 1950's, when the suburb changed from a rural area to a city of 50,000, cannot even now handle the increased number of children. And yet suburban residents are already spending more per pupil than any other group in the nation. In contrast, many more small country schools will be abandoned and replaced by consolidated schools as the number of school districts declines. Within the past two years there was an almost 8 per cent drop in the number of school districts supporting separate schools.

The second major problem concerns school staff. Although today there are over 1.4 million teachers (two-thirds of them women) in the public schools and new teachers are being produced at a higher rate than ever before, there will not be enough teachers to staff the schools in 1970. Competition for college-educated personnel will be cutthroat. The competition will come not only from busines and industry but also from institutions of higher education offering inducements for the recent college graduate to enter graduate work and become a college teacher. Perhaps no graduate today is in greater demand than the mathematician with a doctor's degree. Industry needs him to plan for and program electronic machines, governmental research needs him to supply theoretical possibilities for space probes, universities need him to train other mathematicians, and increasingly high schools need him (even before he completes his doctoral training) to teach the advanced courses now a part of the school curriculum which are outside the competence of most high school teachers. Yet three years ago the graduate schools produced fewer than 250 Ph.D.'s in mathematics and allied subjects and a year ago the total had risen to only a little over 280. In view of the growing need, the number has remained relatively steady, which means simply that competition will be fiercer and shortages greater.

Not just teachers but technical and administrative personnel for the schools also will be scarce. The demand for highly trained counselors and administrators will far outstrip the supply. As the group needing the services increases and the group available to provide those services decreases, education will have to drop its medieval practices.

Effects of Bigness

Bigness in and of itself will produce many changes. Some of them are now evident, some are probabilities, and others are still only guesswork. Perhaps the only certainty is that life in 1980 will differ far more from life in 1960 than does present-day existence from that of two decades ago. Because of these marked differences, the school counselor will experience stronger pressures and new problems and be forced to seek new answers for both himself and his students.

Perhaps of greatest personal importance to the counselor will be the demands within his own profession. To date, suburban schools employ the greatest number of school counselors and this demand will increase. Despite government financial support for the training of school counselors, the shortage of them will grow more acute and pupil–counselor ratios will undoubtedly increase, not decrease. If counselors continue to be trained as at present, the increase in counselors will also mean a decrease in teachers, for counselors are recruited from the present group of teachers.

As the population increases and the move to the cities continues, fewer schools will have a variation in the socioeconomic status of their pupils. Already the suburban communities tend to attract people of like socioeconomic backgrounds. The students in many suburban schools are far more homogeneous in socioeconomic status and cultural values and outlook than are students in the comprehensive high school of the small city. Lacking diversity within the school and the community, the counselor will face even more educational problems than he does today.

Educators, counselors, students, and workers will have a more patterned existence in 1980. More likely than not, they will be apartment-dwellers. Experiences gained from observation and cross-class contacts will be limited. Work will occur farther away from the home and friendships will be established more exclusively within one group. Increasingly, too, both men and women will be working, so that the student with the non-working mother will be the exception, not the rule. Recreation has become more formal as land within the suburbs has become scarcer. Television, undoubtedly in color, will occupy more of the student's time, for he will view it in school as well as during his leisure hours at home. Everyone will have to travel greater distances to find an isolated country spot, for formal resorts and camps will pre-empt available land. *not true in south*

With continuing bigness in industry, more products will reach more homes. Visionaries picture push-button apartments, all air-conditioned, featuring fully automatic cleaners, bed-makers, and cooks. Disposable dishes will even eliminate dishwashers which have to be hand-loaded and unloaded. Solar and nuclear energy will supply electricity and heat and even generate power for the new automobile, monorail, and helicopter. In the midst of automatic, effortless living, more people will undoubtedly engage in do-it-yourself projects symbolizing a return to the primitive. They may, however, be done with less of the zest for a hobby and more of the drive for learning to live in a civilization reduced again to the primitive by the latest form of world-wide destruction.

Again, less diversity and greater sameness will be the keynote of existence. Rapid, inexpensive construction will lead to more buildings in less space mushrooming in the style which Frank Lloyd Wright characterized as an endless row of boxes piled on boxes. Eating and working habits, too, will follow a sameness of pattern as more assembly line goods reach more apartments. Whereas conformity, even now a popular theme for critics, may not reach the proportions described by Orwell and Huxley, it will continue to be a mounting problem as closer living and the vastness of enterprises induce patterned sameness.

Public education, a business now employing over two million people, will of necessity double or triple in size. Necessity will also produce drastic changes in the familiar structure of the schools and colleges and the role of the personnel in them. Currently, changes are only beginning to creep into this, the most traditional of enterprises.

Many changes, both objective and subjective, will occur in the schools and colleges. The most immediate of the objective changes will be the lengthening of the school day and year. Today's educators, anticipating the continuing population explosion, are discussing these two possibilities as means of solving shortages of staff and facilities. Certainly as more people live in cities, there will be less rationale for retaining a school day and term structured so that the youngsters can do chores on the farm and be free for the planting and harvesting of crops. By 1980 a school day incorporating two full sessions and a school year of eleven months will undoubtedly be actualities. Whether the extended school day and year will aid in procuring new staff members is a moot question.

Educators in institutions of higher learning are now debating whether anticipated staff shortages can best be filled by greater use of doctoral candidates for teaching, by stockpiling currently available faculty members, by enlarging classes, by hiring more women professors, by altering methods of teaching, or by some combination of these possibilities. Regardless of the outcomes of the debates, the educational institutions of 1980 will more nearly resemble big business with stringent hours and less time for the "trivialities" of reading and thinking. The trend is already apparent.

There will inevitably be greater reliance upon machines for teaching. The concomitant of machine-teaching is an increasing stress upon "factual" knowledge. Can a subject such as history, essentially nonreducible to facts, be taught effectively by machines? By 1980, however, necessity may have forced the use of machines, whether effective or not. Already television and films are widely used, often not as visual aids but as visual substitutes for teachers. If present trends continue and facilities become more overcrowded, the home living room will increasingly become the classroom and the television correspondence courses will be widespread.

Despite their critics and their shortcomings, objective measures and tests will grow in use and popularity. Bigness breeds short cuts, and objective tests can be machine scored. Increasingly, the teacher will be a lecturer and odious paper work and grading will be relegated to machines. Bigness, as has been demonstrated so often in so many areas, sires impersonality.

Machines may also be used in more creative ways. On cheaper, faster-than-sound planes, students of all ages may be able to participate in the now restricted junior-year-abroad or summer-seminar of travel. The geography classes of the future may be able to visit foreign lands and learn through observation instead of reading about the countries and the people. School classrooms may have to become mobile.

Along with greater use of objective measurement will undoubtedly come an enlargement of the present trend toward selection and segregation of students by ability. The premium on objective intellectual achievement will be higher; the pressures on youngsters for early achievement, stronger; and the age for designating the "gifted," younger. The students' lack of heterogeneous contacts will not be mitigated by the schools.

Curriculum changes will be many. The present curriculum founded on tradition may change both in subject and in content as a new civilization makes new demands on its citizens. The "playing fields of Eton" may have supplied the preservers and protectors of the old world, but the technological and science classrooms will produce the defenders of the new. Learning theory may even be adapted to the curriculum and eliminate outmoded practices. Nursery schools and kindergartens may include such content as foreign languages and science principles for the modern child, already bored with coloring and games by three years of age. Basic anthropology and sociology may be taught before the elementary school pupil has a chance to build in his prejudices. The preservation of society may depend upon such learnings.

Greater specialization will be another objective change, at the same time that specialists will be harder to get. The view of the elementary school teacher as a substitute mother and the possessor of shallow knowledge will die a much-belated and well-deserved death and be replaced by a view of the new teacher as an expert in languages, mathematics, music, or other definite subjects. Each teacher will teach his speciality to more students, probably in ungraded classes. On all levels of education there will be less personal contact and larger classes.[3]

The subjective changes produced by bigness will be less dramatic but equally acute. The student will be forced to do more for himself. At the very moment that the fetish for doing things

[3] The actual size of the "larger classes" will defy the belief of people accustomed to thinking of the average class as 25 to 35 students. At the University of Minnesota in the fall of 1961, for example, 2100 sophomores registered for a single introductory course in psychology. William Johnson's report (*Minneapolis Morning Tribune,* September 26, 1961, p. 1, 6) stated: "There will be no written reports during the quarter and only two tests. Both will be multiple choice and corrected by machines." What is even more shocking is that "there will be two freshmen English classes in Northrop [auditorium] once a week with about 1,900 students in each." College professors commonly complain that their students cannot write; these critics might well start their campaigns for curriculum revision with a study of optimum class size. A student learns to write through practice and careful, detailed individual critiques of his efforts as well as by reading the prose of masters.

to and for the student reaches its peak it will no longer be practical. Particularly in higher education, the return to supervised individual study is evident. More programs of study will revert to the old methods of internship and apprenticeship training. In the world of 1980 the shortage of specialists will be so acute that the students will have to go to the experts and contribute their services while learning. The present practice of stockpiling specialists in one institution and teaching students in a vacuum will be abandoned. One way or another, the student will have to rely on his own motivation, ability, and ingenuity far more than he does today.

Formal classroom learnings will be factual in nature, forcing the student to synthesize and to make applications for himself. If he is not able to do so, he will find help harder to obtain. The high school student of the future will probably be able to solve the differential equation $z(xdx + ydy + zdz)^2 = (z^2 - x^2 - y^2)(xdx + ydy + zdz)dz$ but be less able to discuss the important Platonic questions. He will be trained in the former, but the latter do not lend themselves to the single, right, factual answer.

If present trends continue, still another subjective change will ensue. The student of the future will have less individual choice. As the pace of learning increases he may find more choices made for him at an earlier age, and more of these choices will be irrevocable. In a sense, the student may experience simultaneously greater freedom in the ways he studies and learns and less freedom in the nature of learnings and the uses to which he can put them. He will have to adjust to bigness in school, in employment, and in living and to seek the expression of his individuality in different ways.

Bigness and its effects will also buffet the counselor. Unless he analyzes his role, he will bow to strong pressures for a greater use of the myth of methodological theory and gimmick guidance. Increasingly, he will find himself a test giver, recorder, interpreter, and selection agent—not a counselor. He will be surrounded with all the gimmicks of measurement, information

IBM cards, files, and profile sheets and, wallowing in these, will have no time for individual counseling.

Bigness imposes two important decisions on all school counselors. Working with more students, the counselor must decide whether he wishes to counsel a few students well or steer a large number badly. He must choose between scheduling one or two fifteen-minute interviews with each student or really helping a few. The counselor may delude himself that he reaches all students through gimmick guidance, but such self-deception does not produce effective counseling. Fundamentally, his choice lies between being a superficial adviser or a counselor.

This first decision is important because it underlies a second, even more fundamental than the first. As bigness encroaches upon individuality in all aspects of life, the counselor must decide whether he will support the gimmicks of bigness or the right of each person to his individuality. The decision is patently either-or. In the modern era, the counseling process may be for many students their only opportunity to explore freely their feelings, plans, and ideas and the strongest protection of their individuality and their right to be different. Quite literally, the counselor may be the last stronghold of the individual. But counselors today must make the choice between gimmicks and counseling, between myths and actualities.

Chapter 7

MODERN PHENOMENA IN WORK

A HALF CENTURY ago occupational and vocational experts could view the world of work and be fairly certain that it would not change in the near future. Even then they could not predict with any accuracy what might happen, but at least they could assume that descriptions of occupations would keep pace with developments. Many of the practices and views now labeled mythological had some validity for the period in which they were proposed, and for a nation of 92 million people living in a semiagrarian society relatively untouched by extreme bigness of industry or mass methods of production, transportation, and communication.

In this earlier period, it may even have been possible for a vocational counselor to concentrate upon the specifics of the world of work. In 1910 the various social and psychological sciences had not nullified his view of occupational decisions as intellectual processes, nor had revolutionary changes in scientific and technological fields turned the world of work upside down. Today, however, it is literally impossible for any vocational counselor to keep abreast of more than the broad trends within the world of work. It is useless and delimiting for him even to attempt to do so. With over 40,000 recognized occupations and anywhere from 500 to 1,000 new ones created each year, concentration upon specifics is equivalent to looking at the past. The counselor focusing on the specifics of occupations and the time-worn areas outlined in occupational brochures becomes hopelessly mired before he even begins.

Of far greater value to both the counselor and the student are the distinctive trends within the working scene, the present phenomena and what they bode for the future. These phenomena may be seen in a look at automation, the labor force pyramid, the working woman, the retired worker, leisure, and the resultant changing roles within society.

Automation

The changes in the nature of work and life produced by the first great industrial revolution have been a favorite topic for historians. Many have painted vivid pictures of the fear and hope with which people greeted this development and the new world it produced. Currently, society is undergoing another great industrial revolution created by automation. People fear automation, ridicule it in cartoons, lampoon it on television, experience its far-reaching effects, and hope it will not affect them personally. At the same time they welcome its help in solving problems, use the products it manufactures, and cheer some of its successes. Public reaction is both pro and con. Americans applaud the latest successful missile. Yet the failure of the trial automatic post office in Providence, Rhode Island, was described by one newscaster as a "brilliant victory for the human being over 45 million dollars worth of hardware."

Automation, viewed as either a bane or a blessing, is a necessity. It has made possible, for example, fast telephone service within cities and between far-distant points. Without such mechanical service, there would not be enough telephone operators to handle the calls. Automatic coding of information has produced our modern version of police work, speeded research reporting and communications within industry, and made possible myriad quick services now taken for granted. There are not enough workers available to do such time-consuming work by hand. The complex computers have actually created scientific advances, for they can do in a matter of seconds mathematical problems that would take a trained mathematician years to do —and they are far more accurate. There are not enough trained mathematicians in this country to do the work of even one machine. Translating machines can automatically translate documents from various foreign languages into English and compensate for the current lack of trained linguists. Automation is already a necessary part of the life of every American, for without it the present standard of living could not be maintained.

Just as the phenomena of the earlier industrial revolution created hardships for many people, so has automation. The steel industry alone has spent 7 billion dollars on machines in order to operate at a higher degree of efficiency with some 13,000 fewer workers. Almost every industry is or will be making a comparable change. Who is being laid off? Chiefly the unskilled worker whose productivity and costs cannot compete with machines. The uneducated, untrained worker cannot even be used to "push the buttons" on the new machines, for pushing such buttons is a task far removed from inserting a screw or wrapping a product on a production line. Coding information and programming machines are highly skilled technological work, and the skills needed are growing more complex as advances are made in automation.

Today automation is evident everywhere, from the shop window with its small doughnut-making apparatus, to the ice cream company where one machine does the work formerly done by five or six men, to the large industry where one engineer in a control tower supervises and operates batteries of machines. At times, new types of machines have reduced not only men but also older style machines to the ranks of the unemployed. A current major problem in automation is learning how to speed programming so that the machines will not stand idle.

The fear of automation, once confined to the unskilled and semiskilled, is rapidly spreading throughout the ranks of all workers. Labor leaders fear that automatic typewriters and transcribers will soon make idle vast numbers of clerical employees.

Executives fear that major decision-making will soon be relegated to the computers which even now in many industries not only assemble information but make routine decisions. Computers can, for example, assemble thousands of designs for a plant and rapidly select the best one, saving millions of dollars in time and effort. With information and knowledge virtually proliferating, computers have made possible great advances not only in the physical sciences but in the social sciences as well. Computers can far outstrip librarians and bibliographers in compiling, analyzing, organizing, and reproducing information. Computers can locate, keep track of, and route ships and planes far more effectively than can man. Computers can analyze data, predict the weather, and arrive at complex medical diagnoses. Many an executive, librarian, and analyst is haunted by the fear that someday he too will be replaced by a machine. He forgets that automation can help him and already makes the level of his work possible.

What does the future hold? The picture is increasingly dim for the workers without at least a high school education and some skills. It is increasingly bright for the highly educated, highly skilled worker. As the productive labor force grows proportionately smaller, "thinking machines" may be able to fill some of the gaps, but such machines need educated, trained operators. No one knows what the potential of such machines may be; in fact one of the leading controversies today centers around the question, Can machines think? Are they totally dependent upon the material programmed into them? Dr. Marvin Minsky of the Massachusetts Institute of Technology claims that people too are limited by what they have experienced, and perhaps scientists have not yet learned to program machines properly. The potential to "release magnificent intellectual resources," however, is there. Minsky foresees true thinking machines "probably within our lifetimes, when we can give a problem-solving program the task of extending its own capabilities. What will happen then we cannot guess."

The Labor Force Pyramid

For generations, the portrait of the labor force resembled a pyramid with the unskilled workers, the largest group, constituting the broad base; the semiskilled, the next level of the pyramid; and so up the line through the skilled, clerical, managerial and proprietary to the smallest group, the professional, at the peak. By 1940 the traditional pyramid had begun to be distorted, although manual workers still made up three-fifths of the labor force. Today the pyramid is no more.

As of July 1960, the labor force in the United States totaled a little more than 68 million workers.[1] The distribution of that labor force accentuates some of the trends becoming evident two decades ago. If the trends continue, the pattern of the new labor force will stand out even clearer a decade from now.

Today roughly 12 per cent of the total labor force is in the professional and kindred workers category. Since 1910 this group of workers has shown a steady increase, rising from 4.4 per cent then to 6.5 per cent in 1940. Since 1940 the size of the group has almost doubled.

---

[1] Figures on the labor force vary and can be extremely deceptive. Categories are rarely clear-cut and reflect methods of grouping workers that may not be as applicable today as they were several decades ago. For example, inclusion of farm owners and managers in the broad category of managers and proprietors obscures the basic trend within that group. The largest drop in the labor force has occurred among farm owners and managers, while other managers have increased in number. From 1950 to 1960 farmers showed a drop of about 1.5 million, while the number of other managers increased by 1.9 million. A combination of the two would produce a relatively small rise in the total number of managers. Within the same group, proprietors have tended to decrease—another trend that has been buried by the classification system. Labor force figures like those concerning the work week and working hours are rarely fully defined. Depending upon the source, the figures may or may not include part-time workers. To be completely safe, the counselor must remember that the trends, not the specifics, are important, and that different combinations of figures can prove almost anything. Basic systems of classification are among the most important aspects of statistics.

The largest growth in numbers has occurred within the clerical group. Today it alone constitutes over 15 per cent of the total number of workers, and when combined with the sales group it makes up almost 22 per cent of the labor force.

The proprietary and managerial group has also shown a steady increase, with the exception of farm owners and managers. If one classifies the professional, clerical and sales, proprietors and managers into a white-collar category, this combined group comprises about half of the total labor force. This grouping is slightly misleading because the old concept of white-collar and blue-collar workers has taken on new form. Many of the foremen and service workers of today are more nearly members of a white-collar than a blue-collar classification. Old concepts of categorization do not fit the composition of the new labor force. The old base of the pyramid, the unskilled worker, is rapidly being replaced by machines. In 1960 unskilled workers—the laborers, farm laborers, and private household servants—made up 15 per cent of the labor force. This figure, however, may be misleading, for it includes an increase of over a million women engaged as farm laborers. Any member of a farm family engaged in farm work is included in the Census figures as a "farm laborer." Because every member of a family living on a small farm must work in order for that farm to show a profit, these figures may be skewed. Nevertheless, the group at the base of the pyramid will rapidly decline. In 1910, it accounted for 36 per cent of the labor force; in 1940, over 25 per cent; today, only 15 per cent.

Twenty years ago, predictors of trends estimated that within two decades the semiskilled workers would probably surpass in percentage growth the clerical and sales group. Viewing mass production within industry, these prognosticators did not take into account the far-reaching effects of automation. The rapid acceleration in the number of semiskilled workers in the 1940's leveled off and then began to decline. Although the semiskilled constituted a little over 21 per cent of the labor force then, today the percentage has dropped to slightly over 20 per cent.

Interestingly, the semiskilled category is largely made up of the unskilled who advance to semiskilled and the skilled who take semiskilled or operative work to remain employed. Technological changes have tended during the past decades to obscure the old distinctions among unskilled, semiskilled, and skilled workers.

Today's picture of the labor force exemplifies clearly the important trends. The untrained, unskilled worker is increasingly finding his services unneeded. On the other hand, all white-collar workers are in greater demand, particularly the professional and technological ones. Moreover, most professional, managerial, and clerical workers work in urban areas and ever-increasingly work for someone else.

The continued growth in population and in big business and industry means that the size of the group at the top of the socioeconomic scale will increase. Alba Edwards contended in 1950 that the general socioeconomic trend of the labor force was upward. The 1960 figures seem to attest to the validity of his statement.

The Working Woman

Generalized figures about the labor force do not mirror one important phenomenon that has far-reaching effects. Perhaps the most important trend within the past twenty years is the growing number of women in the labor force.

Women have always been a part of the labor force. In 1870 almost 2 million women comprised roughly 15 per cent of the total working population; in 1910 over 7 million women worked, 20 per cent of the total; by 1940 there were almost 13 million working women, a little over 24 per cent of the total. Today this group numbers almost 23 million and constitutes over one-third of the total labor force.

Even this picture of growth does not indicate the rapid increases within the past few years. Employment, particularly of *married* women, has risen so markedly that now this group accounts for three-fifths of the total growth in the labor force.

The nature of jobs open to women has also changed radically. In 1910 about 42 per cent of the working women were unskilled; in 1940, 25 per cent; and in 1960, 11 per cent. The percentage of women in the unskilled group has decreased more rapidly than that of men. The detailed occupational breakdowns of the 1950 Census revealed that women were working in each of the 446 listed occupations. Clerical occupations still employ the greatest number of women, followed by sales, teaching, machine operating, bookkeeping, food service, and nursing. Certain occupations today are almost completely "women's work," since 90 per cent or more of the people working in them are women: professional and practical nursing, dressmaking, telephone work, housekeeping, secretarial work, library service, millinery, dietetics, medical and dental office work, and private household labor. The occupations in which better than half of the employees are women make up a long list.

Within the past ten years women have managed to find more jobs open to them in all the occupational groupings listed in the Census. While the increase in the number of women employed in clerical and service occupations has been highest, the most interesting steady increase has taken place in the professional and managerial occupations. Today over 11 per cent of the working women are employed in professional and about 9 per cent in managerial areas. The upward socioeconomic employment trend for women is marked.

Rosie the Riveter, and Bella the Belle of the Belt Line became popular stereotypes during World War II. Predictions then were that the Rosies and Bellas would return home after the war or at most stay on in operative work. Some Rosies did, but many returned later. Today the majority of working women fall into two groups, the young unmarried, and women of whatever marital status in the thirty-five to fifty-five age range. Women in all socioeconomic classes work.

Many reasons are offered for the current phenomenon of the working woman. Modern appliances, packaged foods, ready-made clothing have eliminated such old-time chores as home canning, baking, sewing, weaving, and candle-making and have literally freed the woman from her home. Nursery and other schools as well as social agencies help solve her baby-sitting problems. As her family's standard of living rises (and every family can afford new products on credit), she works to pay for luxuries and for the education of her children. Whereas only a few women found a high school education possible a half century ago, today the median level of education for women is higher than that for men. Many modern women, finding time on their hands in apartment life, seek work as an escape from boredom.

Perhaps, however, the most common reason for the great numbers of working women is necessity. As education and training become more important assets, the educated, trained woman finds hitherto closed doors opening to her. Today few school boards refuse to hire a married woman teacher. The hitherto masculine domains of taxi-driving, plumbing, printing, and soldiering now have female incumbents. Even women engineers are finding new doors open to them. The law of supply and demand has to a great extent created the phenomenon just as it created Rosie and Bella.

If current trends continue, the school counselor will have to consider seriously the concept of the working woman. He can no longer assume that the girls he counsels will work only until they are married and then stay home and rear their children. Nor can he assume that the occupations open to women are those for which training is quick and easy. The probabilities of careers for women—married, unmarried, widowed, or divorced —are actualities which the counselor will have to recognize.

The Retired Worker

Today's school counselor working with teen-agers tends to feel removed from the modern phenomenon of the retired worker. At times a student's questions about various retirement plans and social security benefits may seem to the counselor simply a projection into the future. And yet the joint phenomena of retirement and the retired worker have strong subtle effects upon the entire working scene.

Societies have always faced a problem of what to do with their members who are no longer productive. Only a few basic solutions have developed. Some oriental societies established a tradition of reverence and support for the aged, usually the largest nonproductive group. Most other societies, however, have solved the problem by either isolation or death or some combination of the two. The American Plains Indians often either abandoned the aged members of the tribe or buried them alive. Not until modern times, however, has the problem of what to do with the aged reached large proportions, because most people did not live to an advanced age. Today with life expectancy rapidly rising and soon to reach the high seventies and early eighties, the problem of the aged is real and immediate. Thus far, the solution seems to be a slightly more humanitarian adaptation of those used over the centuries. Modern Americans employ retirement and isolation.

Often forgotten in modern society is a basic question, Who is aged? The American Indians established a flexible classification. Usually any member of the tribe no longer able to keep up with its migrations or to contribute to its life in some way belonged to the aged and was a person who drained off supplies but could not contribute. The specific age was usually not even known, and was far less important than the individual functioning of the person.

Today American society has different answers to the question, Who is aged? The man of forty-five who seeks a job and cannot find one because of his advanced age views himself as "too old." Increasingly, old age begins at retirement and, as businesses and industries grow larger, retirement no longer is a matter of choice for the employee. Company policy establishes a set age, popularly sixty-five, and democratically everyone regardless of ability, training, physical or mental health, and usefulness leaves the company when he reaches that age. Henry

Steele Commager, attempting to predict the future, sees the retirement age eventually lowered to fifty. Even today, either a man or a woman may now begin to draw social security benefits before age sixty-five.

The continual lowering of the retirement age is particularly interesting in the light of modern scientific discoveries. Geriatricians point out that the actual physical process of aging begins in the thirties and proceeds at various paces and in sundry ways. Some people at sixty-five are physically and mentally young; some are not. In some people, the characteristics commonly associated with age—wrinkled skin, gray hair, and baldness—may be present, but the arteries, mind, and stamina may be those of a comparatively youthful person. Individuals differ widely with regard to aging.

Increasingly, geriatricians are stressing two points. Modern medicine has delayed the process of aging, but modern views often hasten it. The person's own view of himself, others' views of him, and all the psychological adjustments the person past sixty-five must make either slow or hasten his deterioration and his idiosyncratic process of aging. Science and technology have advanced, social treatment of the aged has not.

The problem of what to do with the aged is less troublesome in a nation of small farms and small businesses than in a predominantly urban one of large businesses and industries. There are chores and work that older people can do on farms. The individual owner of a small business can choose for himself the hours he will work and the age at which he feels he is no longer able to perform his duties. He can find something constructive to do. He may face the great problem of where his money for retirement is coming from, but he does not face with such stark reality the endless span of idle hours.

In an urban, industrial economy the problems are greater both for the society and for the individual. Usually a man does not judge the age at which he reaches a point of nonproductivity. His retirement age is set. His retirement benefits are usually sufficient to take care of his basic needs, but more often than not he is literally reduced to finding nonproductive amusements for himself. He is an unnecessary member of society, and he knows it.

Within the past two or three years, only one real solution has come to the fore—the ancient one of isolation. Many large cities are now setting up special housing projects for the retired, to supplement such older establishments as nursing homes and old people's homes. These new projects have their own medical staffs, shopping centers, and recreation facilities, emphasizing games and hobbies designed to fill the idle hours. Some groups of retired people are setting up for themselves small communities limited to those no longer deemed valuable to society. The result is that the bridge between the productive and the nonproductive, between the valuable and the useless is growing wider. If present trends continue, the people over sixty-five in America will eventually live in an isolated society of their own.

Everywhere the emphasis is upon youth. Even politicians, judges, consultants, and college presidents, those representatives of work formerly looked upon as strongholds of the older segment of the population, are now recruited from the ranks of people in their thirties and forties. Aged individual creative artists find working opportunities and public reverence awaiting them. A Toscanini could be a sought-after conductor until his death; a Picasso, an ageless artist; a Robert Frost or a Carl Sandburg, a poet and lecturer in demand until the end of his days.

Some college professors also find constructive outlets for their abilities in opportunities to work as visiting professors or lecturers in colleges and universities here and abroad after they have been retired from their regular posts. For years, many "aged" professors have been doing notable work on the staffs of colleges in Africa, India, Afghanistan, and other distant points, although they have been turned out to pasture as too old for their own institutions. In the modern era of science and youth, however, only individual, already established, creative men of letters, music, and art, or professional men are presumably worthy of esteem and use after they reach an age when the social security checks start arriving.

The subjective effects of compulsory retirement are many and far-reaching. They permeate all age groups and tend to combine with other forces in society to produce some of the fundamental changes on the working scene. Today the effects of compulsory retirement upon the working man and the prospective worker are almost as direct as upon the retired.

The first subjective, subtle effect is the heightening of the pressure upon the worker in his early and middle years. He tends to feel that if he is not well on his way toward success by thirty-five or forty at the latest, he has lost his chance for real accomplishment. After forty he is hesitant about changing his field of endeavor or even his place of work. Unless he is well-known and highly successful, he finds any change almost an impossibility, for he is already too old. Hence he stays where he is and begins to look forward to remaining with the same company until he retires, whether he is satisfied with or successful in the kind of work he is doing. The older he is, the stronger the pressure becomes.

Subtly, an attractive retirement plan and the irrevocable process of aging cut down on the exploratory experiences of workers. Even the person in the thirties with ten or fifteen years invested in the retirement plan of a single company thinks twice before he moves. Although he may be dissatisfied, he has too much invested in his future retirement to be able to start over. Security and investment literally outweigh striving for satisfaction. More often than not, he becomes a new type of marginal worker, putting in his time and performing his tasks without real interest, involvement, or motivation. In business and industry, seniority protects him from dismissal; in educational institutions, tenure. The creation of the new marginal worker is the second subtle effect.

The third is a shifting of goals for the older worker. The man or woman of sixty or even younger begins to prepare for retirement and looks forward to many years of not working. The strong pressures for middle-age accomplishment have made the worker focus upon his job, devoting in many instances far more time to it than his official working hours would indicate. Suddenly the work to which he has devoted most of his waking hours exists no more. What he will do with his time is his major problem. It combines with the many psychological effects of being unwanted and useless to stimulate a shift in goals. The worker focuses upon retirement and strives to make enjoyable a period of idleness. Rare is the individual worker facing retirement who views this period as one of constructive pursuits. He seeks merely something to do to forestall and combat boredom and idleness, and these goals are negative in essence.

The effects are evident not only upon the middle-aged and near-retiring worker, but also upon the youthful prospective worker. The fourth effect is a heightening of pressure upon this group. Perhaps some of the current popularity of mythical vocational guidance theory and practices arises from this pressure. The youngster making an early, wise vocational choice can focus his attention on one field; prepare for it thoroughly (and such preparation means a late entry into the labor force, since preparation too is an elongated period); and work for accomplishment early because the time left for success is continually being shortened.

Company policies of employment and retirement help to create the pressure. Many trained workers today make their first job choice not only in terms of salary and the challenges the job offers, but also with an eye upon the amplitude of the retirement benefits. The man of twenty-five in 1970 will probably face and have to prepare for thirty-five years of work and twenty years or more of idleness. If current trends continue, the period of idleness will eventually equal the period of productivity and the pressures will mount. The youthful worker even now faces both a world of work and a hitherto unknown world of idleness.

There are undoubtedly many reasons for the rise of pattern theories during the past decade. Not the least of the reasons is probably a covert, psychological one—the periods of growth, exploration, establishment, maintenance, and decline and the ages assigned to them reflect well present trends within the world of work. Whether these periods are natural to modern man and should be promulgated is a question rarely discussed. The theories mirror what is happening. Unfortunately the mere statement of the theories seems to foster and to lend credence to the belief that the outlined stages are typical and that they occur at specific ages. Their growing recognition creates simultaneously an acceptance of the patterns outlined and a reinforcement of them. Certainly some men begin a period of maintenance in middle life, but whether and how much the structure of the world of work forces this period upon them is unknown. Neither physiological nor psychological studies constitute the basis. How many men might work constructively far past retirement is unknown, for few of them today have the opportunity to try.

Theoretically a period of retirement without financial worry is a halcyon time, and for some people it actually is. But for many more people it is not. Many retired people refer to themselves as having been "put out to pasture." The horse, once his working days are over, seems to enjoy being free to frolic across the greensward, but horses are not people. A man's needs do not change automatically at sixty-five and revert to a level of physiological necessity. All the needs ranging from belongingness to self-actualization continue, and they can rarely be satisfied by restriction or pointless endeavor.

Within the next few decades much attention must be directed toward the realism of retirement policies and the effects they produce throughout all age groups. Centuries-old methods may not be applicable to the modern day, and yet the ancient method of isolation is at present the only solution. In fact, never before in history has the isolation of the aged been as widespread and dramatically enforced as it is now in the United States. The problem affects not only the retired, but all age groups. The

nation suffers great losses when creativity and constructive enterprise become the exclusive province of youth.

Leisure

The fifth great modern phenomenon associated with work
concerns new concepts of leisure. Increasingly, books and articles discuss this modern development; counselors and educators
worry about the worker's constructive use of his extra leisure,
without wondering whether it is mythological or real.

Statistically, Americans have at their disposal more leisure
than any other group in the history of western civilization.
Their working day and working week have shrunk. The logical
conclusion is that the time spent not working is free time which
can be devoted to leisure. Modern life, however, tends to falsify
the age-old subtraction method of arriving at amounts of leisure.

Statistically and actually, two groups in modern society have
more leisure than ever before. The people who are automatically
retired at sixty-five have no working hours, and neither do the
youngsters who have not yet reached the age of sixteen or so,
when state law permits them legally to seek employment. These
two groups have much idle time, but what happens to the leisure
of the rest of the population?

For many people, the work week may be a statistical nine-to-
five set of hours, with an hour off for lunch and two days for a
relaxing weekend. Most Americans employed full-time, however, work not a thirty-five, but a forty-eight hour week.[2] Furthermore, as the jobs at the upper end of the socioeconomic scale
increase in number and those at the lower end decrease, the specific, designated work week becomes a myth. The young executive wishing to get ahead works not only the thirty-five hours
demanded by the terms of his contract, but also vast amounts
of overtime often unremunerated. He, like the teacher, takes

[2] Official statistics on the "average work-day" and "work-week" include
part-time workers. Hence the averages are always less than the actuality.

work home and often spends evenings and weekends preparing reports. He also spends evenings entertaining, not for relaxation but for business. These hours, however, are not a part of his official working week.

As cities grow in size, transportation to and from the place of work also consumes its share of the leisure hours. In and around the largest cities, it is not uncommon for individuals to spend one to three hours each day commuting to and from work. The commuter's transportation is not much more effective in proportion to the distance covered than that used by his ancestors. Even the commuter who drives his automobile to work fights his way through traffic and sometimes requires more, not less, time than his counterpart might have needed riding a horse. The earlier commuter also faced fewer problems parking his horse than today's commuter does with his automobile.

Further incursions into leisure are made by the popular practice of "moonlighting." Many working people hold two jobs, one during the day and another at night. The skilled operative may be a gas station attendant in the evenings; the teacher may man a paramutual window at night during the racing season; the clerical employee may be a salesman on Saturdays; the executive or the college professor may teach an extra course or do consulting work during his "free time." Each person has his own method of supplementing his basic income and adding to his working hours. Moonlighting is such a frequent practice that many businesses and industries have set up rules defining the extra jobs that are acceptable or not. Governmental employees often campaign to obtain the right to engage in moonlighting.

Another modern phenomenon further diminishes leisure: the working wife. Modern appliances and frozen foods may have freed the woman from her home, but they seem to have freed her not for leisure but for work. Well over 50 per cent of the women working today are married. Hence in families where both the husband and wife work, they share in running the household. Much of the leisure of both is devoted to the tasks that even the new machine cannot do, such as shopping, running the machines, and cleaning the house.

Perhaps the most fallacious assumption is that a statistic about working hours tells something about the intensity of the work. Certainly automation has helped to create the record heights in productivity per man-hour of work, but even running machines today is no easy task. Somehow many people assume that the work involved in sitting at a desk is less taxing and strenuous than that done by the man who dug ditches twelve hours a day. Certainly it is physically different, but undoubtedly many times as productive of tension and anxiety. Various researchers who have tried to work out equivalents, have suggested that five hours of mental labor are more taxing than ten hours of physical labor done by someone who is physically fit. There is, however, no definite way to equate the working hours of the modern man with those of his earlier counterparts.

The difficulties faced in the actual spending of leisure also distort the statistics. The man seeking an evening or a day of rest and relaxation at the ball park or the beach or the theatre must first get there, usually through streams of traffic. Then he has to return home through more of the same. As cities and suburbs increase in size, his recreation and entertainment spots get farther away and he spends proportionately more time and effort to secure his relaxation.

Not only commuting to work at an office but also the more extensive travel which is part of some types of employment cuts into nonworking hours. The average American travels more than 10,000 miles a year. The salesman who covers a large territory may work officially only five days a week, but his Sundays may be spent in traveling long distances so that he may start work in a new locale on Monday. The executive may fly thousands of miles each week, chiefly during the evening hours and on the weekends, to attend company meetings or to check plants in different sections of the country. Necessary travel appears far more often in the statistics of the expense account than it does in the tabulations of working hours.

The many factors of overtime, commutation, moonlighting, working wives, intensity of work, and travel tend to make a myth of leisure for the working man during the height of his productive years. He may feel guilty because he seems to have so little leisure, when all reports indicate that he should have so much. Actually he often has the right merely to grimace and mutter, "What leisure?"

Perhaps the greatest problem today regarding leisure is that very little is being done to prepare the populace for its use. The greatest amount of leisure occurs after retirement. What happens to the man along the way? As a youth, he engages in supervised activity, usually in groups. Then after he finishes his education, he plunges into years of whirlwind activity during which work is predominant and leisure is largely a myth. Then suddenly he must prepare for endless hours of leisure although very little in his background and experience has prepared him for activities unrelated to business. Increasingly, even the occasional round of golf the working man manages to squeeze into his schedule is not played for the activity itself, but rather to meet people who might be helpful to him in his advancement in his job. The purposes and nature of the leisure activities he engages in during his youth and working years are far different from those of the post-retirement era.

The activities of his youth were designed for youth and for groups. The activities of his working years were predominantly those of a spectator or of a businessman. Leisure was not a monumental problem, for he literally had very little, regardless of the statistics. At retirement he has to shift to inactivity. Purposeless, newly learned hobbies, television, spectator sports are often idle ways to spend idle hours. Constructive use of leisure is one of the major problems of modern civilization.

Changing Roles

The modern phenomena of automation, a new labor force structure, the working woman, the retired worker, and the myth of leisure blend to produce deep and far-reaching changes in cultural roles in the United States. Many of the traditional views of the roles appropriate for American citizens are being shattered to such an extent that the culture today's youth share is indeed far different from that their ancestors anticipated.

Perhaps the most overt change in roles has occurred because of the growing number of working women. Among the younger married couples, the working wife is now commonplace. Originally this phenomenon was viewed as a temporary necessity, and both wife and husband assumed that the woman's place is in the home and that she would return there as soon as her extra salary was no longer needed. Today, although many people still hold this view, what actually happens is this: the wife takes time off from her work to bear children and then returns to the labor force.

The modern working woman has been cast in a new role. In ever-growing numbers, she is a person highly trained for her work, and increasingly that work is of a technical, semiprofessional, or professional nature. Hence she becomes not a temporary member of the labor force working for a supplementary income, but a competitive member striving for status, prestige, recognition, more money, promotions, and executive rank. She tends to feel that she should use her talents and abilities, and that housekeeping and child-bearing and child-rearing do not offer her adequate outlets for self-actualization. More and more modern women are indeed direct cultural descendants of their earlier prototypes who campaigned for temperance, suffrage, and birth control, but today's crusade is not marked by placards, parades, and male laughter. The inroads are too deep. The modern crusade takes place more subtly in terms of competition, ability, necessity, and a shift in roles.

The pervasiveness and effects of a shift in male–female roles can readily be seen. Popular magazines contain many articles about the shared responsibilities in marriage, about the joint duties of husband and wife when both work. Columnists dole out advice about joint bank accounts, and recipes for men who do the outdoor cooking. Psychologists describe the broadening role a man must play in rearing his children, and prenatal clinics teach him as well as his wife how to prepare the formula, feed the baby, and change the diapers. Pictures of men hanging up their drip-dry shirts, or operating the washing machine, or running the vacuum cleaner are no longer rarities. In idle conversation, men compare their adeptness at housework, while a woman whose work is in the home feels almost apologetic as she identifies herself as "just a housewife." She may add (as if to justify her existence) that she does a great deal of charity or club work. In America, both men and women have assumed new roles and identities.

With the increase in automation, a complete reversal of role often takes place. The laborer unable to find a job takes over the household responsibilities while his wife becomes the breadwinner. Unfortunately, the values of such a man make him less able to adjust to this acute change in role than is his better-educated counterpart. He finds himself losing the self-esteem that working brings and the male identity that being the support of his family carries. Often he finds release from his degraded position in the only outlets left to him—alcohol, antisocial acts, severe and unreasoning discipline of his children, and the production of a large family. As employment opportunities become scarcer for the unskilled man, the problems caused by the abrupt change in role will increase. Housekeeping duties and welfare checks are in modern American civilization stigmata on the traditional male identity.

A second shift in role deals with a concept of the ideal man. Today the respected person is educated and does not work with his hands. The role of the educated person is far different from that of the earlier frontier ideal. Only today is this shift really coming to the fore, for only within the past decade or so have the majority of the workers in this country come to be in the white-collar category. Increasingly, the prestige attached to the skilled trades is falling, and the vocational type of education and training is the province of the youngster who cannot learn the academic subjects. Subtly the role of the blue-collar worker is one of a second-rate citizen, and the divisions between the non-college and college segments of the population are ever broadening.

Frontier traditions die hard, and the return to the traditional view of the American male is currently vicarious. From the comfort of an easy chair, the typical American views his frontier prototype on the television screen. He engages in the traditional work activities only in his leisure. He may fulfill his new modern role by do-it-yourself projects around his house, building his recreational toy—a boat or a trailer or an outdoor fireplace—taking his vacation in the great outdoors, shooting at small and large game, trimming his lawn, traveling to unfrequented places, cooking his meals on rustic equipment, or collecting the relics of his progenitors. Only in an avocational way can modern man re-enact his traditional role. In his vocation he must play a new one—that often referred to as the man in the grey flannel suit or the organization man—if he is to match the current ideal.

The third great change in role occurs within a definite segment of the population. This change involves directly the older members of the population as they shift from useful to useless citizens. In the current emphasis upon youth, the oldest members of the population perhaps suffer the greatest indignity of all, being tolerated. There is nothing more outmoded than the retired person, be he an ex-president of the United States, an ex-board chairman, or an ex-plumber. His methods, ideas, views, and values are from the past and, except as a primary source for historical materials, his usefulness is over. No change in role is more swift or acute or complete than that any person undergoes as he passes into the magic age of retirement.

The fourth shift in role is perhaps the most pervasive, for it touches all age groups within the population. It is the subtle shift from man as secure to man as insecure. One quality pervades the modern scene and the modern phenomena in work —change. Today, nothing in the world of work can safely be viewed as static or traditional, except perhaps the people who write about it. Change brings with it fear, for the unknown is always a source of trepidation.

Much of the twentieth century has been marked by a striving for security. Unions grew powerful because workers wanted the security of better wages, seniority rights, and guarantees of employment; educators fought long and hard for tenure; products were sold with money-back guarantees; people died in wars to make the world safe for democracy. Many modern critics deride what they see as the overintense yearning for security in the younger generations. And yet, in the mid-twentieth century, two factors have seemingly swept away much of the hard-fought-for security. Within the broad picture, the atom, hydrogen, and neutron bombs have combined with space travel to demolish the old views of the world and to make total destruction an imminent prospect.

Within the job picture, automation has fulfilled a similar role. Fear and insecurity characterize many workers today as they see old jobs disappear and know themselves to be unqualified for the new ones. An informal survey by reporters from *The New York Times* points out that fear is greatest among the workers with the least amount of seniority, but widespread among all workers, for no one is sure what machines and computers will eventually be able to do. Within one insurance company, for example, "$8,000,000 of data-processing equipment does everything but attend a policyholder's funeral with insurance check in hand." [3] Whose job will disappear next is not an idle question.

The fears associated with automation have blinded many people to the hope that change also brings. While individual workers will undoubtedly suffer from the economic upheavals that leave them unemployed, those same changes are opening up new opportunities for qualified workers and broader vistas of greater productivity and challenge. The electronics industry, practically unknown two decades ago, is now the fifth largest in the United States. The International Business Machines Corpo-

[3] *The New York Times,* April 7, 1961, p. 16.

ration is now a world-wide operation with five times as many employees as it had a decade and a half ago. Research into the ocean depths is just now developing into a science of oceanography promising a time when mining and farming will take on new shape and methods on the ocean floor. Occupations are no longer encased by the atmosphere above the earth or limited by the water surrounding the land.

These facts, however, are cold comfort for the person facing the direct insecurity of change or unemployment. The new world often demands new skills and flexibility that the worker does not possess. For many, the shift from security to insecurity is paramount.

No one can ignore or dismiss as transitory the modern phenomena in work. Basically they affect the roles and values of everyone. With change the only constant, the modern counselor must look to new concepts of his work, to new practices, and to the world ahead.

Chapter 8

SPECIAL PROBLEMS RELATING TO WORK

THE MODERN phenomena in work combine with the current trend toward vast change to create special problems relating directly to work. In a sense these are also some of the major social problems of the present scene, for three of these special concerns are familiar to any reader of a daily newspaper—the problems of youth, the unneeded within modern society, and minority groups. Not so familiar is another problem that heightens those facing these three groups—that of current methods of employment.

Social problems do not lend themselves to easy solution, particularly in an era of rapid change, because attitudes and values are slow to alter. People often seek to solve these problems by trying to speed up or slow down the changes. Social scientists, for example, complain that technological developments outstrip social changes and that the latter do not occur rapidly enough. Many other adults, on the other hand, reminisce about the good old days and state firmly that there would be fewer problems if changes were slower in coming or if there were a reinforcement of the attitudes and disciplines of the past. Teen-agers, meanwhile living in their own present world, usually grumble that no members of the older generations understand either them or their society. Seemingly change is always too slow, too fast, or misunderstood.

The modern counselor cannot take refuge in any of these views,

146

for the special problems relating to work are an intimate part of his job. He must be aware of the problems and make certain that his values and views do not lead him into snap judgments, regression to the past, or misunderstanding. The problems of the adolescent as the potential worker, of the enlarging group of the unneeded, of minority groups, and of current methods of employment are everyday actualities to the understanding school counselor.

The Potential Worker

An increase in the number of people involved always seems to magnify the size of a problem. Today there are more teen-agers than ever before—almost 13 million of them in the fifteen to nineteen age group and 16.5 million in the ten to fourteen category. The number of young people tends to focus attention upon them.

Furthermore, much more is known about the adolescent group today than about any similar group in history. Researchers study their attitudes, habits, and skills; school officials test their aptitudes, interests, achievement, and personality; policemen keep track of their crimes and offenses; statisticians in insurance companies compile figures on how the adolescent drives. All kinds of reports about adolescent behavior reach the public. The most alarming of the reports tend to be most widely publicized, for news—whether in the newspapers or on television or radio—seems to be news only if it is alarmist in nature or spectacular in some way. The adolescent who murders, robs, or rapes is far more likely to reach the front-page headlines and the national television report than the adolescent who wins a scholarship or never has an accident. The result is a distorted picture of adolescents.

Still another factor enters. To a greater degree in the United States than in any other country, a cult of adolescence has been created and promulgated. Certain problems are expected of all adolescents. Youngsters in this age group do have problems, the normal problems of growing up, but these problems are so well known that they have almost become a point of concentration.

Not only emphasis, but also the manifold pressures upon youth today heighten these problems. Perhaps the most insidious of these pressures are those for early decisions, early and high achievement, and early success. Adults somehow expect adolescents to speed up the process of maturity. Undoubtedly the adolescent today is physically bigger, better educated, and wiser in many ways than adolescents of any generation before his. He has a better diet, and more opportunities to learn and to keep up with current happenings all over the world. Whether and how these advantages affect the age-old process of maturing is not known, but the youth who *looks* like an adult is expected to *be* an adult in all ways, and these expectations work additional hardships upon him. Many times adults castigate youngsters for not performing like grownups, and expect from them a maturity not even typical of their elders.

The cult of adolescence has produced another strange effect. Parents and teachers and even some counselors, familiar with the problems of youth as they have never been before, have a tendency to dismiss these problems as the normal ones of "growing up." The youngster is going through a phase which, given enough time, he will eventually outgrow. The effect is that adults many times dismiss the adolescent's problems as unimportant and temporary. At the same time, parents and school personnel, busier than ever before, seem to have less time for real communication with young people. Listening takes time.

During the next two decades the problems of adolescents will inevitably mount, not decrease. The small percentage of adolescents now engaged in crime and delinquency will rise. As city living becomes the mode, as people are crowded closer together, as pressures mount, as expectations rise, as personal communication lessens, and as differences in value systems become sharper, antisocial behavior seems to increase.

The school dropout, for example, has problems that do not

lend themselves to easy solution. With the accent on intellectual achievement and the world itself an intellectual frontier, he does not have the equipment to fit easily into society. He cannot readily find work, regardless of how much he wants to work. The jobs he might find tend to be dead-end. He seems to be rejected on all fronts. He cannot easily return to school, for there too his role is doubly hard—again he is rejected. The chances are great that he is retarded in his skills, probably more as a result of his values, background, and experiences than as an outgrowth of lack of innate ability. But the attitudes of other people do not distinguish between the two. He faces a bleak world and he receives little help in understanding either it or himself.

The employment outlook for the school dropout will grow worse not better. Gone are the days when the boy dropping out of school could find ready employment in mining, construction, heavy industry, or transportation. With much competition, jobs go to the most experienced and the most highly trained. The outlook for the girl dropout is slightly better than for the boy —some of the girls find clerical and operative jobs; most of them find employment as waitresses and household servants. Automation and increased productivity per man-hour of work indicate that the school dropout will continue to face a dismal employment scene. And yet the dropout rate continues to be between 40 and 50 per cent of the students enrolled in public schools and will probably decrease only to about 35 per cent by 1970.

Increasingly the recent high school graduate also finds stiff competition when he seeks employment, for he too is an untrained and inexperienced member of the labor force. The fact that the high school graduate has less trouble finding a job than the dropout reflects the value of the diploma. Whereas only one out of eight high school graduates could not find work in 1959, one out of four dropouts was unemployed. Increasingly, the inexperienced youth will be competing for fewer and fewer unskilled and semiskilled jobs against a group of unemployed, experienced workers. Even today employment opportunities in these categories are scarcest for the fourteen- to nineteen-year-old male applicant. The unemployment rate for this youngest group is three times that for the group thirty-five to forty-four years old. Clerical, sales, and operative jobs are being filled by girls whose high school training more often includes the necessary skills and whose wages are often less than those offered boys. Occupations for which high school graduation once provided entry now require college graduation; types of employment for which a B. A. degree was sufficient now demand graduate work. As the level of education rises, so do job requirements. It is commonly and truly stated that today the high school diploma is the "selling" equivalent of the eighth-grade education a generation ago and the college degree, of the high school diploma of the past. Interestingly, even in a time of high unemployment, only one out of fifty professional or technical workers is out of work, a figure that includes those voluntarily seeking other employment.

The special problems of the potential worker neither begin nor end with his difficulties in finding employment. Many of his most immediate problems are intimately bound up in the psychological effects created by the modern world. No less troubling is the fact that the subjective psychological effects of change create both problems and challenges.

The first effect is brought about through better systems of communication than have ever existed before. Previously motion pictures, newspapers, and periodicals led the way in setting up stereotyped ideals for youth; now television has reinforced those other media. The stereotype of the American female and male may be seen at any hour of the day or night—the Marilyn Monroe or variations of the same theme; the tall, slim Western hero or private eye. Frequently these stereotypes combine to form the American couple in a luxurious apartment or a traditional vine-covered cottage with all modern furnishings and equipment and two children, preferably boy and girl. These characters become the image of the ideal American, and adolescents compare themselves and their parents and homes with them.

In a nation without counterbalancing heroes, stereotypes become even more effective. Today's society does not produce or stress individual accomplishment except in the creative arts, and creative artists have never been American heroes. Even the flight of the first astronaut into space did not create an individual hero, because the effort was that of an extensive and coordinated team—and teams cannot become heroes. Rather, part of the American ideal today is to produce a citizen who can fit effectively and modestly into a team whether in business, industry, research, or exploration. It is not strange that modern society has also created the juvenile gang, a means for rejected youngsters to satisfy not only a need for belongingness but also an antisocial replica of the "team" approach, marked by delegated specialized functions and coordinated attack on a problem.

Modern advertising carried to the public by all media not only creates stereotypes but also works on fear and guilt. Its effectiveness can be seen by the fact that the younger people in society are the ones advertisers are attempting to corral. The basic themes are simple. Unpopularity is the result of body odor, unmanageable or mousy hair, halitosis, and a long series of other offenses against the social code set up and delineated by the advertisers. Certain products can distinguish the user as a person of taste, charm, prestige, sex appeal, and success. The result is a stereotyped American striving upward on the socioeconomic scale, safeguarding himself against the common societal offenses. The youngster who is unpopular or cannot match the common stereotypes finds his rejection reinforced, for gradually and pervasively advertising has created a singleness of image.

The result of all the effects of communication is to heighten feelings of inferiority in the youngster. Not many adolescents can duplicate the appearance of the select group pictured on screens in front of them every day, despite the use of all products from A to Z. Not many youngsters can live the idealized life they see constantly portrayed. Not many of their parents resemble the prototypes. At the same time, they find no specific individual models of achievement to imitate. With the spread of middle-class values, even their own parents want their children to do "better" than they have done—but "better" remains a nebulous concept.

The second effect is that at a time when society stresses creativity, the youngster of today has fewer opportunities for individual endeavor and is handicapped by a stereotype of the value of the good team man. Much more is done to and for the youngster than at any time in history. His ball parks, tennis courts, swimming pools, and playgrounds are not only laid out for him but peopled by coaches to guide him in an activity and by social workers and recreation directors to insure his cooperative participation. He plays a game that is already set up according to designated rules fairly enforced by an adult. In many ways he is expected not merely to be a participant but to learn to do things the right way and to develop expertness. Gone are many of his opportunities to engage in the creative endeavor of building the diamond and measuring it for himself, devising and bickering over the rules, discovering the swimming hole and building the diving board or raft, and finding out for himself the joys of creative enterprise and participation. Perhaps the most important aspect of creative activity is no longer possible, for now the equipment is there and the rules are taught. In a sense, recreation has become big business. Whether it produces more creative individuals or even experts is a moot question.

The third effect of modern society is a lack of outlets for hostility and escape. The youngster in a large city usually lives in an apartment or a crowded area. Pressures pile up and he seeks an outlet. He has difficulty in finding an isolated spot where he can mull over his troubles. He has even more difficulty in finding an outlet for his hostility. If he kicks a stone or a can along the sidewalk, a policeman stops him, for he might injure a pedestrian. If he starts a fight on a school or public playground, the supervisor stops him. If he argues during supervised games, he is likely to be labeled a poor sport and to receive a lecture on how to play the game according to the rules. Even within his own apartment, he cannot make too much noise, because the neighbors might complain. When something hurts him, the youngster of today can neither fight back nor cry—one is prohibited by law, the other by the social code that says such action is unmanly.

There are today fewer definite things against which to rebel. A generic "they" not an individual represents authority—the "theys" of government, administration, management, and beliefs. Even parental authority has been replaced by democratic process. Individual action appears less effectual amid a large number of people. The individual attempting to rebel finds not only fewer distinct objects of rebellion but also fewer definite causes to espouse, and thus suffers an ignominious end. He is not a rebel with a cause subject to the heroic fates of legendary heretics, but rather he receives the appellation of eccentric or nonconformist and is dismissed as a persion without good human relationships.

The fourth effect of present-day society is widespread rejection of youth in ways that are detrimental to the youngster's view of himself and his abilities. Many youngsters are finding vast differences between what they read about the modern world and what they experience in it. The challenges it presumably offers to the young seem to lose something in the translation, as youth look for the intellectual challenge and atmosphere of learning in college or the opportunity to put creativity to work in industry. At the same time that pressures demand early accomplishment, youngsters find the way to accomplishment lined with rejection or boredom.

Many able high school graduates find the ultimate in rejection when they apply for college entrance, for no problem is more acute for today's student than getting into college. Increasingly, college admission for the student depends upon his high school average and his ability to perform on standardized tests—unless, of course, he happens to be a gifted athlete. Whereas even ten years ago many eastern colleges and universities accepted one out of every two applicants, today they are turning away three out of every four and, in some institutions, nine out of every ten. This practice does not mean that the rejected applicants are not college material. Ten or twenty years ago the rejects might have become the college graduates.

In view of the fact that almost every institution of higher education is concentrating upon "skimming the cream" off the group of applicants, another problem accompanies the first. The percentage of students from each entering class who actually gain a college degree has not altered significantly since the early part of the century. And yet, theoretically, the freshman group of students in most colleges and universities is the most scientifically select that has ever existed. High school counselors and administrators have faced the fact that special grading systems must be used for accelerated classes of the gifted. Obviously, college faculty members clinging to the sanctity of the "normal curve" have not questioned whether such a system can apply to a select group which is in no way a random choice from the population as a whole.

For two groups of youngsters, the dropouts and the creative, societal rejection is the most severe. Jacob Getzels' research highlights the fact that teachers tend to like the youngsters who score well on group tests of intelligence and to dislike the creative youngster, who is often a disrupting influence in the classroom because he questions analytically or seeks to establish new relationships. Even the tests presumably geared to select the "gifted" are gradually being viewed as doing a better job of selecting the conforming student of high prosaic achievement than the creative youngster. The stress in big business upon the team approach and the good organization man results in further rejection of the young creative person. The rejection of the dropout is overt and definite; the rejection of the creative is covert and subtle. One is as effective as the other, and society is the loser.

The major social problem concerning youth is how to help youngsters withstand the pressures and rejections of society. Certain forces dictate early accomplishment and simultaneously offer fewer outlets for creativity. The modern scene is increasingly bleak for those youngsters whose talents do not equip them for life on the new intellectual frontier. How to train and to utilize what present society rejects poses one of the greatest problems for the next two decades.

The Unneeded

The older people whose services are no longer needed might be called the "unwanted" but their work and effort were once valued. Today, however, there is an increasing group that might well be labeled the "unneeded," comprised of people who have never had the opportunity to find themselves and their services of value to society. They are tolerated, even cared for, but they are simultaneously unnecessary, and often a drain on societal resources.

Many diverse people make up this category of the unneeded. The most easily distinguished are all those persons whose physical handicaps limit them to special institutions for the handicapped or whose early training has been such that they have never had the opportunity to learn to operate at least semi-normally despite their handicaps—the victims of cerebral palsy, the deaf, the mute, the blind, and the severely crippled. The fringe members of the handicapped are those with minor physical defects or nonvisible disabilities whose employment opportunities are limited by the inability of the person to pass the health requirements set up by large industries. Despite many research studies which point out that absenteeism is often less among these fringe people, their employment opportunities are far fewer than those for the healthy. To a certain degree these fringe people are also in the group of the unneeded.

The handicapped may or may not overlap the second large group of the unneeded, the mentally retarded. Often placed in this group are all those members of society who are unable to function at an established learning level in the early years of life and school. Such people are unable to learn simple mental tasks and to deal with abstract concepts. Some others, because of emotional blocks or other impediments to their learning, may also be classified with the mentally retarded. Whatever the cause, the mentally retarded make up the second group of the unneeded in modern society.

Increasingly throughout the twentieth century another group has joined the ranks of the unneeded, all those persons whose lack of education and training has made them virtually unemployable. Not unwillingness to work but lack of skill and training has made them public charges and cast them as completely as the handicapped and the mentally retarded into the broad category of the unneeded.

The groups of unneeded share several characteristics. First, the size of each group is constantly growing. Modern medicine has prolonged the life of many handicapped persons whose disabilities date from birth or early childhood. It has also added many persons to the ranks of the handicapped. The victim of a heart attack, serious accident, diabetic coma, or epileptic seizure that might once have been fatal can now be treated effectively. Yet employment policies have not kept pace with medicine. At the same time, automation has removed the jobs once open to the unskilled and even to the mentally retarded, so that continually the group of unemployables is enlarging.

The second common characteristic is the simple one of being unemployable for whatever reason. In one sense or another the unneeded become public responsibilities. Some are institutionalized; some band together and form their own methods and places of employment; some with high degrees of training find individual kinds of work; others draw unemployment, relief, or welfare checks. The member of the unneeded who can be totally self-sustaining is rapidly becoming an exception.

The resultant third characteristic is a loss of self-esteem and self-respect. In American culture, one indication of maturity is independence expressed not only in a degree of self-sufficiency but also in the materialistic form of being able to find and to hold a job, of being able to supply one's own food, shelter, and clothing. In turn, the successful holding of a job is a source of self-esteem to the individual. The working person has proved his independence, fulfilled one of the basic requirements for membership in a contributing society, and gained societal acceptance and the respect of his fellow human beings. Increasingly this minimum requirement for maturity and citizenship is no longer available to the unneeded, and the aid extended in terms of welfare or special work is more often than not an inadequate substitute.

One of the major problems within the next two decades will be the constructive utilization of the unneeded. Some gains have been made in relaxing the employment policies of major industrial concerns so that the nonseriously handicapped can find employment. Many members of this group are highly trained and can easily become excellent contributors. The object in this case is a comparatively simple realistic lowering of employment barriers. The solution for other members of the unneeded is not so simple.

In the modern era of automation, real employment for some of the unneeded is at best a long-range project. Those born with physical handicaps need special training to reach a degree of physical self-sufficiency. Those already mature and untrained need a process of re-education and training that will enable them to become contributing members of society. Thus far, the types of training offered too often exist only in fields already outmoded by the very development that created the unemployment in the first place. Solutions are not easy and they are not to be found in attempts to turn back the clock and reinstate outmoded methods of production. They must be sought in terms of the world of the future, not the past.

Minority Groups

Women in the labor force are the largest minority group, but there are many other minorities distinguished by factors other than sex. At various times in the United States, almost every national group has found itself "the minority" in certain regions or cities. These groups were designated by such collectives as the Swedes, the Irish, the Poles, the Italians, the Germans, and often by less flattering terms. People view as minorities those persons who are visibly different—Negroes, Orientals, and American Indians—those who speak a different language; those who attend a different church; those who cannot meet ideal health requirements and the many with nonvisible handicaps; and those labeled artistic, intellectual, retarded, gifted, or creative. Depending upon his own origins, section of the country, and experiences, everyone has his own view of what a minority group is, who belongs to the minority, and who is suitable for what kinds of employment. Each person has his own set of biases that make such factors as sex, national origin, appearance, language, religion, health, and intelligence important to him in a positive or a negative way.

Many studies of minority group problems have appeared during the past decade. These as well as the available statistics make possible several generalizations which every counselor working with minority group members should keep in mind.

The first generalization is that each new minority group usually finds employment at the bottom of the socioeconomic scale. Each new group of immigrants found entry into the labor force through unskilled jobs. Meantime, the previous minority group members moved up to higher rungs on the ladder. Even today in the large cities this trend is evident. The Negroes, long a minority group in New York City for example, are finding semiskilled, clerical, and sales work openings, as the Puerto Ricans move in to take over the fast-disappearing unskilled jobs.

Generally speaking, as new groups move in, old ones move out. This statement is as true of employment as it is of housing. Certain jobs and occupations become so intimately associated with a minority group that they become the "work" of that group. Many Southerners have for generations divided work into that proper for Negroes and that for white people. Specific occupations become the province of one sex. Men were the original nurses, secretaries, bookkeepers, and elementary school teachers. As the minority group, women, moved into these lines of work, the men moved out and men's work became women's. The men, in turn, retained as predominantly men's work the positions of higher pay, prestige, and responsibility in allied fields—hospital administration, medicine, office management, accounting, and school administration. Currently, as more members of the unskilled and semiskilled groups are seeking training and upward movement, men are again beginning to enter such professions as nursing and elementary school teaching. Demarcations of work are continually shifting as one group replaces another on the upward climb.

As a new minority moves in, its members are judged most harshly and with greatest prejudice by the group they are displacing. This generalization is illustrated both on a large scale and in minutiae. Historical studies of western civilization point out clearly how often the persecuted, after achieving acceptance, become the persecutors. The Christians, once thrown to the lions by the Romans, stamped out with bloodshed and militarism all pagans and heretics. Those who worked hardest for *liberté, égalité, fraternité* sired the Reign of Terror. The Negro in New York City castigates the Puerto Rican, resents his invasion of Harlem, and suggests that "this country should be for us good Americans." The earlier German or Scandinavian immigrant objects strenuously to large numbers of Italians or Balkan Jews. Women administrators rarely hire women to work for them. The minority group member often finds the least acceptance where he might expect the most.

The fourth generalization deals with unemployment. Minority group employees will be the first to lose their jobs in times of recession. Far more women teachers than men lost their jobs during the 1930's; far more Negroes than white people are laid off during the minor "downturns" in the economy. Security in employment is always more precarious for members of minority groups.

The fifth generalization is closely related to the fourth. The minority group member has to have advantages that offset his minority status. He has to have better education, training, job performance, and attendance in order to compete with other employees for promotions and salary increases. He also has to be markedly superior to other applicants in order to obtain the job in the first place. A double standard operates. Some forms of it are overt: many companies always give larger increases in salary to men than to women; many schools and colleges have different salary schedules for men and for women. Distinctions by race and religion are generally not so overt. Some companies and educational institutions adhere closely to unwritten quotas: only a certain percentage of the employees or students may be Negro, Chinese, Catholic, or Jew. Occasionally a company or an institution may employ a minority group member with qualifications inferior to those of other applicants simply because he is a member of a specific minority group and will constitute a token gesture toward broadmindedness. In general, however, the minority group member experiences more frustration in getting ahead than does the majority group member. The person from a minority group must be better in order to stay even.

The fact that necessity opens many educational and vocational doors is the sixth generalization. Legislation and theory may supply the stimulus, but the need for certain types of employees furnishes the opportunities. When mathematicians are needed desperately, fewer employers demand specifics by way of sex, race, religion, or health. When typists are in short supply, acquaintance with a typewriter far outweighs other considerations. When a small community seeks a physician, training and willingness to come are far more important than whether the new doctor will be the first Negro or Oriental member of that community. When the employer has a choice among applicants, minority group status may be the deciding factor, but need for and scarcity of employees remain the chief determinants of opportunity.

Increasingly, minority group members are urban dwellers. The Negroes, once primarily an agricultural people, have moved in great migrations to the large urban areas in the North, Midwest, and South. New minority group arrivals tend to settle in urban areas in coastal and border sections of the country. Hence the seventh generalization is that minority group problems will no longer be restricted to a particular section of the country, but rather will focus upon the major urban areas. Friction about school zoning ordinances and segregated housing is commonplace in many urban areas, regardless of the section of the country. Population increases, intensified competition within restricted areas, shortages of facilities—all will heighten the problems.

Perhaps of most intimate concern for the school counselor is the last generalization: youngsters who are members of minority groups often have their normal problems of growing up intensified by their minority status. Often the recipient of ridicule and rejection, the minority group youngster develops heightened feelings of inferiority. Operating from a background of values and motivations far different from those of the average middle-class youngster, the minority group member fights intensified problems of being different, that greatest of youthful "sins." He may react to his own feelings of inferiority and difference by extreme responses either of passivity or of aggression. Many times, his needs for information and skills are greater than those of the majority. Every person must learn to live with, accept, and understand himself. Self-acceptance and understanding often pose greater problems for the minority group student.

Within the next two decades many opportunities will undoubtedly open up for minority group members who are educated and highly trained. The unskilled minority group member will face monumental problems, for he will compete at a disadvantage with other unskilled workers.

Methods of Employment

The special problems of the potential worker, the unneeded, and the minority group member are often multiplied by the methods of employment they must go through in large businesses and industries. As places of work increase in size, the methods of employment of workers tend to become more formal and to be

handled by a personnel department set up for that particular purpose. The number of employees engaged in personnel work
varies but, in a medium to large business or industry, includes
specialists in testing, job description and analysis, recruiting,
labor relations, interviewing, general counseling, retirement counseling, and employee investigation, as well as all the medical
staff comprising the usual health services. Personnel work, too,
has become "big business."

Personnel departments in industry are a relatively new development, dating back only to the early 1920's. Since then they have
come to be a major and integral part of business and industry.
Their purpose is to make "scientific" the procedures of selection
and promotion. The growth of personnel departments has been
so rapid that, like vocational guidance programs, they rarely un-
dergo evaluation and they often employ questionable tools and
methods.

The normal procedure for hiring employees in a large business
or industry is far from simple. Suppose a new job is created in a
department of a large company. The department manager writes
a description of the type of person he would like to employ.
Normally a new typist will have to be a high school graduate,
able to type a required minimum number of words per minute,
and possess such usual characteristics as cooperativeness, initiative, and pleasing personality. If the job is totally new, chances
are that the first requirement will be a college degree in some related subject. The manager will usually want a young, healthy,
experienced employee. The manager's requirements are the bases
for the job description and may or may not have any relationship
to the qualities the job actually demands.

The manager's write-up of the type of person desired goes to
the personnel department. There, special investigators analyze
the job, classify it according to its rank in the total company picture, assign a rank and salary to it, and publicize the opening.
The completed job description and analysis then go to special
interviewers, who do the initial screening of applicants, matching
qualifications with those judged essential for the job.

Occasionally all the candidates, but more frequently only those who passed muster on the first interview, go on to testing. Many personnel departments give a myriad of tests. The candidates for the typing job may have to take a short paper-and-pencil intelligence test, a clerical test, and a typing speed test. Frequently, they may also take some short personality test and various aptitude tests. One law of the personnel departments often operates: the higher the level of the job, the more tests the applicant will have to take. The prospective executive trainee will be given batteries of tests—even his wife may be invited to take a group Rorschach.

The testing program is the second weeding-out step. Additional interviews follow, the number of them depending upon the importance and complexity of the job. The normal length of time consumed in filling a job may be anywhere from one month to several months. Naturally, if the typist is needed in a hurry the procedure is shortened and the first candidate who appears and can type is hired. Then the testing program is done ex post facto in order to keep the records straight.

Many times the penchant of the personnel director adds complications to the usual methods of hiring. Some executives may prefer graduates of large colleges, some of small. Some may encourage the hiring of minority group members, others may discourage it. The original company interviewers usually know and take into account these unwritten parts of the job description and add still others of which they may or may not have been aware.

One way or another, getting employed is now a complex job virtually demanding special training and skills. William H. Whyte, Jr., in *The Organization Man* highlights many of these skills and includes a special section on "How to Cheat on Personality Tests." Writing a personal résumé is an art in itself. Many employment agencies devote considerable time to helping the job seeker compose a résumé and learn to sell himself. As more people move to urban centers, youngsters have to be skilled in test-taking, résumé-writing, and interviewee techniques in order to compete successfully in the job market. School counselors have to be acquainted with the trends.

The direct result of the formality engendered by the growth of personnel departments has been twofold: a general upgrading of job requirements and a greater rigidity in hiring practices. In describing the sort of employee they would like to have, most employers jot down the easiest requirements first, the educational ones. The odds are that the messenger boy or girl in a large company will have to be a high school graduate. The probability is high that the first requirement listed for a job on a higher level will be a college degree. Regardless of the type of job, the person who scores highest on the tests will probably be hired. These practices lead to strange results. A college graduate scoring high on an intelligence test may be engaged to do pedestrian work. The high school graduate demonstrating the greatest amount of measured ability may be hired as messenger or machine operator.

It is not uncommon to find that jobs formerly demanding a high school graduate, now prefer or even require a college graduate. Many times the nature of the job has not changed, only the entrance specifications for it. This upgrading of requirements occurs particularly during periods of recession and is seldom reversed. The previous secretary in a company may have been a high school graduate; when secretarial applicants are many, the newly-hired secretary may have had two years of college or may be a college graduate; gradually college training becomes a requirement for secretaries within that company.

Perhaps the greatest change has come in one of the areas where an acute shortage exists—engineering. A frequent complaint is that a degree in engineering is a requirement for employment in many technical jobs that could as well be filled by noncollege graduates. A 1960 survey by Deutsch and Shea, Inc., revealed that much of the job dissatisfaction of engineers results from factors centering around possible boredom: excessive paper work, routine, and lack of responsibility and authority in their work. Interestingly, this dissatisfaction is voiced at a time when, according to the Engineering Manpower Commission of the Engineers

Joint Council, the median salary of all engineers is at a new high, $9,600 per year. Despite the profusion of graphs, charts, and statistics common in all personnel departments, there are literally no thorough studies of what educational requirements are necessary for what jobs. Whereas some of the current man-power shortage of highly trained personnel may be real, some of it may exist because of the whimsical upgrading of entrance requirements for jobs.

The second result is steadily increasing rigidity within the employment structure of large companies. A frequent complaint from young job seekers is, "How on earth can anyone have a college degree, ten years of experience in a single field, and be below thirty years of age?" In a similar manner, the older worker mutters, "I can't afford to leave my job. Who will hire a man past forty?" The requirements laid down in job descriptions limit employment to specific groups except in times of emergency. Company investments in pension and medical benefits tend to work hardships on older or handicapped workers, and dictate the common requirements that the beginning employee be below forty or forty-five and in excellent health. The upgrading of educational and experiential requirements limits the youthful job seeker's opportunities for employment and promotion.

Within the next two decades, employment practices will have to be scrutinized to determine how much and in what way they contribute to unemployment among the less educated and to shortages among the highly trained. Upgrading and rigidity create as many problems as they solve. If present trends in employment practices continue, the productive group within the population may be limited to the highly educated between the ages of twenty-five and forty-five.

The Broad Problems

The many special problems relating to work have broad implications in terms of their effects upon people. Transitional periods always make for unsettling, parlous times in a psychological sense, and the modern scene is certainly no exception to this generalization.

To the youngster, the handicapped, or the minority group member seeking employment, the modern working world can often loom only as a source of confusion. He knows that in times of labor scarcity he finds great flexibility in hiring practices. Personnel departments waive requirements. In times when labor is plentiful, he finds only great rigidity. Often the rigidity becomes so extreme that he may wait months to hear whether or not he is going to be employed—in many cases he never does hear.

The effect upon the members of the special groups is particularly severe. For months, or even years, they can read about acute shortages of employees in a particular field and yet find employment closed to them. The methods of employment seem to them to be shrouded in mystery and confusion, and the personal results cause continual intermingled anger and frustration.

Much of the frustration arises from the discrepancies between the information supplied to the potential worker by his vocational counselor and his actual experiences in seeking employment. He has been told that he must make a wise, intellectual decision about a field of endeavor and prepare himself for it. He has undoubtedly been tested to find out what field might best suit his aptitudes and interests. In fact, he might, if he is one of the unemployed, have been tested and advised not only by his school counselor but also by an employment service counselor or a rehabilitation counselor. Too often the potential worker finds, however, that the very decisions these counselors have forced upon him narrow his opportunities, for he cannot find employment in the field chosen for him. In these rapidly changing times, some particular types of work no longer exist. The job seeker vents his anger and frustration against all around him and feels that his chances for fulfillment are gone. More often than not, when he does secure employment in a field chosen for him, he finds that his interests have changed and that he is becoming an increasingly dissatisfied employee.

Too often one rule operates. The person who has great difficulty finding employment is less likely to feel free to leave a job that he dislikes. Since being able to support oneself is a source of self-esteem, many individuals are willing to suffer endless boredom and the lack of opportunities for self-actualization rather than once again to be without work. As rigidity increases, more people will join the ranks of the confused, disillusioned, frustrated, and angry. The sobriquet, the angry young man, is a very real part of the modern scene.

The second broad problem is growing impersonalism in education, business, and industry. At the turn of the century, impersonalism in these institutions was viewed as a major problem. The size of the problem has not diminished but rather has become a semiaccepted concomitant of bigness. The acceptance of it has not lessened its effects, merely the attempts to cope with it.

Interestingly, many of the solutions to impersonalism have actually heightened its effects. The personnel departments set up to serve the employee as well as the company have often produced added barriers to employee–management communication and introduced rigidity into hiring practices. Similarly, in education greater reliance upon school grades and objective tests as a means of college admission have not insured the entrance of the "best" people into college but have enhanced the impersonalism of the process. Dependence upon objectivity in an attempt to be fair has introduced the impersonal element into areas in which subjectivity is an essential.

No problem in America today needs more thorough re-examination than the many practices set up to solve impersonalism. The next two decades may not result in the automatic world portrayed by Orwell and Huxley but the trends are there. Somehow today's personnel and admissions officers feel more secure basing and justifying their decisions upon highly questionable objective evidence than upon the soundest educated guess. The long-range result is a group of people unwilling and unable to take a chance. Just as the frustrated employee dares not leave his unsatisfying job and risk getting congenial work elsewhere, so also the careful official dares not make decisions unless he is buoyed up by all possible objective data. There may be times in the future when the nation will need people unafraid to stick their necks out and eager to act on the basis of what they themselves know and believe.

The third effect of the special problems relating to work is a growing discrepancy between the values relating to work long held by Americans and the values being put into practice. Not the least confusing elements in the modern world of work are the inconsistencies in beliefs most people encounter. The great concern of many professions for a clear delineation of ethical and nonethical practices is one manifestation of this confusion. Great arguments ensue in terms of teaching values in schools, for traditionally schools should be those impossible establishments, valueless domains. The result is that old values have disappeared and new ones have not been adopted to replace them, for no area is less discussed today than that extremely troubling one of values. The school counselor cannot, however, shrug off this concern, for nothing is more integrally bound to his work.

The school counselor, the student, the worker—all are caught in the confusing middle ground between myths and actualities. The same myths that dictate the counselor's training and practices envelop employment procedures in business and industry and admissions practices in colleges and universities. People and the nation they comprise suffer the consequences of living with myths and unexamined problems in terms of confusion and frustration. Who will be able to break the stranglehold of the myths? This is one of the most challenging questions of the next two decades. Perhaps only the force of actuality and societal needs will accomplish the task when the trends apparent today become the actual world of work tomorrow.

Chapter 9

VALUES RELATING TO WORK

Since time immemorial, work in some form has been a fundamental part of every adult's life. Through work, adults have acquired status and recognition as well as material rewards. Little by little, certain values developed relating to work and its place in the lives of men and women. These traditional values, modified only slightly through the years, still influence the reactions, feelings, and attitudes that Americans express about work.

Today these values are undergoing considerable re-examination and modification because of the kinds of lives people lead. This re-examination is neither deliberate nor in many cases even conscious, but it seems nevertheless to be leading to new trends in the ways people regard work and view themselves as workers. The traditional values and the modern trends in values combine to make up the values relating to work.

Traditional Values

In our country, the traditional values relating to work are a heritage from the Puritans, who presumably conducted their lives according to them. The rigors of frontier life did nothing to ameliorate the harshness and rigidity with which the Puritans applied their standards to themselves and others, and some of their sternness persists today in American judgments about work.

Work is good, while pleasure and frivolity are bad, sums up

169

much of the Puritan attitude toward work. Over the years, Americans have become more lenient in their attitudes toward pleasure and have come to look upon it as a welcome and healthful change from work. To some extent, pleasure is regarded more favorably because it prepares one to work better and harder. Americans are still skeptical of frivolity, however, and tend to regard it chiefly as the province of the young and the light-minded. Work remains the one great good, and people who do not work are viewed with some contempt, faintly tinged with envy. Even artists and writers, whose places and times for working are irregular, are regarded somewhat askance.

Because work is good, men are obliged to work, and more especially to work hard. According to the Puritan ethic, it is not sufficient to do just enough to get by. Rather, the individual is expected to put forth his maximum effort on all tasks at all times. Hard work is the duty of every man. In the Puritan view, no one works for fun or because he enjoys the job he is doing—in fact there are hints that the enjoyment of work is odd or even sinful. Man works because it is his duty to God, and little attention is paid to the fact that without work man might not eat. This view of work as service to God rather than service to self permeates many American attitudes toward work and provides a rationalization for some of the selfish reasons why men work.

Since work is man's duty, success in work is evidence of God's favor. And success for twentieth century Americans, as for the Puritans, is measured in terms of money and property. The man who fulfills his duty to God by working hard and exercising thrift will be able to exhibit the marks of God's favor in his bank account, the property he owns, and his income tax returns. Success is judged not in terms of enjoyment, contentment, or satisfaction, but in terms of tangible wealth and property. Holding this value, Americans always find it difficult to explain how a man can be industrious, thrifty, and unsuccessful; or the converse, lazy, profligate, and yet well endowed with worldly goods.

A natural corollary of these values is one that exalts perseverance. The man who sticks to a job or a task is the good man, and his efforts will eventually lead to success. Today perseverance is a rather old-fashioned term, and Americans talk about job stability and job persistence rather than the old Puritan virtue, but the value is the same. The man who sticks to the job is good, while the man who flits from job to job or changes his field of endeavor—regardless of his reasons for doing so—is bad.

To these basic Puritan values, Americans added others, which were the natural outgrowth of their experiences in a new and sparsely populated country. In a frontier civilization a premium is attached to the ability to do things for oneself—build a house, till land, track game, and protect the property that becomes the reward of this ability combined with industry, thrift, and perseverance. For most Americans, working was and still is equated with doing. The man who works does something, often with his hands, but not always. The man who works has something to show for his efforts, even though it may only be a stack of papers read or a pile of memos dictated. Thinking is not working, nor is dreaming, even though the thoughts and the dreams may lead to developments and products of lasting concrete value. Work, however, is doing, and the man who sits staring into space is not working.

Closely tied to the concept that work is doing is the idea that work must have a utilitarian outcome. Work should lead to a useful product, something that can be eaten or worn or lived in or used in some way to lighten work or to make it more efficient. According to this value, the writer, the artist, and the musician are in some way less productive people because their creations are not utilitarian, but serve the purpose of pleasure and esthetic enjoyment. To some extent, these creative artists are viewed as tempting man away from his duty to work and toward the sinful enjoyment of pleasurable experiences. Although Americans have moved away from the extreme application of this value, many vestiges of it remain in their attitudes toward the artist as a worker.

Education, too, must have a utilitarian value. Children go to school and are taught the things they will need to know in order to become workers as adults. They are encouraged to take the subjects that will be useful to them either in getting a job or in getting into college, where they will repeat the process in terms of future work. Americans have little or no concept of a student studying a subject for the sheer joy of learning. Even teachers justify their subjects in terms of their usefulness in later life—the Latin teacher advocates the study of Latin on the grounds that it will aid in the pursuit of a medical career or improve one's odds on standardized vocabulary tests. Education must have a useful purpose, and the study of even the most *outré* subject must be rationalized by dredging up some reason why it will serve well the future worker.

These, then, are some of the traditional values relating to work. They color to a considerable extent the attitudes of most Americans toward their work and that of their neighbors and friends. In the period since World War I, some modification and distortion of these values have become evident, but the traditional values remain the cornerstone of American thinking about work. They rise to haunt as well as to help those who strive toward new standards suited to a changing world.[1]

Modern Trends in Values

Americans have not discarded the traditional values, but they seem to be modifying those concepts in terms of a new era and new social conditions. To some extent, people today are becoming a bit cynical about the Puritan values and their meaning in twentieth-century life. In a society which protects its citizens from

[1] The reader will find interesting comments upon values in general in all of the following: Crane Brinton, *A History of Western Morals* (New York, Harcourt, Brace, 1959); Roger Burlingame, *The American Conscience* (New York, Knopf, 1957); and Max Lerner, *America as Civilization* (New York, Simon & Schuster, 1958). Although drastically overdrawn, *The Freudian Ethic*, by Richard T. La Piere (New York, Duell, Sloan & Pearce, 1959), presents a thought-provoking point of view.

womb to tomb, how worth while is it for the individual to practice industry and thrift? In an economy featuring installment buying and planned obsolescence, why save for the new car or the dishwasher and postpone the satisfaction that can be had today? In a society that clings to the Puritan definition of success, why not acquire the trappings of success as easily and quickly as possible?

Although success is still defined in Puritan terms, the road to success is not. Industry and thrift receive lip-service, but today success justifies almost any means. Where success requires good team membership, men bury their individualism and become good group workers. When success requires one to be a politician, men play company politics with all the concentration and desperation of which they are capable. And some settle for the trappings of success—the home in the suburbs, the right car, the essential appliances, the proper clubs—and the bills and insecurity that go with not knowing where the next payment will come from. Many of the ways in which men work for success are in conflict with the teachings of the Judeo-Christian tradition and the Puritan values, and this conflict taints the material success of many individuals with a sense of guilt.

Essentially, Americans are working for success when they do not know what it is. In a society in which money is relatively plentiful and property fairly easy to obtain, a definition of success in terms of those assets no longer suffices. But if money and property do not define success, what does? Some people have tried to make satisfaction in the job a criterion of success, but the idea of happiness and pleasure associated with work is foreign to the traditional values. For too long, Americans have tended to think that the man who is achieving material success through his employment is *ipso facto* deriving satisfaction from his job. Hence they have no concept of satisfaction with which to augment or replace the old definition of success. Happiness, enjoyment, and contentment in connection with work are too alien to the traditional values associated with work to permit their easy assimilation into a new concept of success. The old idea of work as a duty to God overshadows even today the possibility that work might be a pleasure to man.

Lacking an adequate concept of success, Americans find it equally difficult to distinguish the kinds of men whom they will admire, applaud, and reward. In terms of the traditional values, clergymen perhaps merit the plaudits more highly than any other group, but certainly today no group is more unapplauded or under-rewarded. Similarly, the man who works hard, is thrifty, and dutifully renders service to his Creator should be admired and deemed successful—and some are but many are not. Actually Americans seem theoretically to value one type of person and to reward and respect another.

In the matter of rewards, other traditional values exert considerable influence today. The stress upon work as doing and upon education in its utilitarian aspects has led Americans to their present attitudes of suspicion of the intelligent person and semi-scorn of advanced education except as it can be expected to increase future dollar income. Currently, people are beginning to recognize the value of higher education, the importance of thinking as contrasted with doing, the need for basic research in opposition to applied research, and the service of which the creative individual is capable. This recognition, however, has yet to affect in any significant way the rewards Americans offer to the men who perform these functions or to alter appreciably the honors accorded to them. Research scientists are still viewed as odd individuals who are necessarily antisocial, while university professors are considered either inept or definitely "touched" because they prefer teaching to industrial work. The creative child who asks awkward questions or arrives at devastatingly logical conclusions remains the teacher's *bête noire* and receives not rewards but suppression. Faced with the menace of Communism and haunted by the specter of total annihilation, Americans have begun to recognize the importance of some of the qualities not included in the traditional values, but this recognition has yet to be incorporated in the sets of values upon which most Americans base their actions.

Today Americans seem to be starting upon the long process of rebuilding their value systems to include some of the qualities and kinds of men that current civilization seems to require. The well-educated man, the creative man, and the research man seem about to come into their own and may in time be judged on their own merits rather than viewed in terms of the stereotypes fostered by the traditional values. But Americans still cling tenaciously to traditional values even as they remold them. Today's revision of values centers around the scientific areas from which Americans can expect tangible utilitarian results. Financial support is given to medical and other scientific projects, and praise and honor go to Dr. Salk and Dr. von Braun. Even the support given to guidance had for its purpose the identification of the gifted student and his early cultivation. Americans still do not reward to any great extent their poets, historians, writers, artists, or musicians. The immediate utility of any activity remains one of the most important of all values.

American values, then, are in a state of flux. People cling to the old and the familiar at the same time that they recognize the need for the new. But change comes slowly and with great difficulty in the area of values, and only time and a continuing need will teach Americans to appreciate the many kinds of people, their varied talents, and the idiosyncratic contributions they can make. Even harder to learn will be the appreciation of the many kinds of behavior these individuals will exhibit as they work and play. Should Americans value the good organization man or the individualistic man or both? Can the country afford to accommodate both kinds of behavior? Can it afford not to? Most difficult of all for Americans will be to recognize and learn the worth of the nonutilitarian contributions to life. When Americans can agree that the artist works as hard as the plumber, the poet as hard as the lathe operator, and the writer as hard as the executive, and reward them accordingly, the re-examination of values will have made great progress. But that day, if it ever comes, is far in the future.

Meanwhile the transitional state of the values relating to work makes the tasks of the counselor trying to help students with educational and vocational planning extremely difficult. In the midst of widely differing sets of values that are themselves undergoing change and modification, and dealing with many individuals, all of whom differ in a variety of ways, the counselor has little to which to cling in his work with students. Over the years he has been taught to adhere to the values implicit in the concepts of vocational guidance, but in a world of changing values even those of vocational guidance are not immutable.

Values of Vocational Guidance

Vocational guidance developed against the background of the traditional values of American society and incorporated them into its basic concepts. Work is good and it is man's duty to work are basic tenets of the vocational guidance expert. While God is not usually mentioned explicitly in the credo of vocational guidance, the specter of an implacable, wrathful Creator is implicit in much that vocational guidance workers say and do. Much that is Puritanly repressive hangs on in the attitudes and actions of the vocational guidance experts.

In general, vocational guidance workers subscribe to the middle-class values. They tend to stress industry and thrift and the other Puritan values. In addition, they expect students, regardless of their backgrounds, to plan in long-range terms and to be willing to postpone satisfactions until some distant future. Vocational guidance workers encourage striving and applaud the youngster whose planning shows a willingness to strive and a desire to advance socially and materially. Like most Americans, vocational experts define success in materialistic and status terms and tend to look not at the satisfaction to be derived from the job, but at its monetary and prestige rewards.

With the changing standards since the two world wars, vocational workers have to some extent modified the values implicit in their work. Currently they are placing a higher value upon education. Whether this evaluation has really been internalized by the vocational guidance people or whether they are merely paying lip service to one which society constrains them to accept is a moot question.

Vocational guidance workers are also emphasizing early achievement both in the academic and in the career areas. Youngsters must start early in school to get the good marks that will allow them to progress from one educational level to the next and eventually into the one "right" job. Little attention or emphasis is accorded the fun of learning or the personal importance of becoming a cultivated person. Similarly, early achievement in work is receiving greater emphasis as vocational guidance workers become immersed in the current cult of youth.

Since the advent of Sputnik, vocational guidance workers have incorporated into their values one which overemphasizes the importance of science. The youngster who is interested in and adept at scientific studies seems somehow to be more worthy of attention and special help than the one who likes drama or the social sciences. Naturally this value stems from the prevailing emphasis upon things scientific within the culture as a whole, and vocational guidance workers cannot be expected to remain totally aloof from the tenor of their time. Nevertheless they have demonstrated a notable lack of the ability to examine and analyze the current values in terms of the effect upon their work and upon the students with whom they work.

In conjunction with the value exalting science, vocational guidance people also subscribe to one that requires talented youngsters to make use of their talents for the good of society and the country. This, of course, is an old Puritan value in another guise. Duty to work is no longer a religious duty, but has become a patriotic one; the force impelling men to use their abilities is no longer fear of and respect for God, but respect for the dictates of society and fear of annihilation. Certainly, able students deserve the opportunity to develop their talents and to use them, but do they have the right to use them in ways which are suitable for themselves as individuals although not always in accord with the contemporary dictates of society? Do students have a right not to use their talents? These are questions that most vocational guidance workers would find it easy to answer in theory, but impossible to implement in practice simply because they are immersed in the values of their society and yet relatively unaware of what those values are.

Not unexpectedly, vocational guidance workers also support the current and traditional view of success as defined by wealth and possessions. They steer youngsters toward the occupations that will allow them to achieve the outward forms of success, and they discourage students from entering those fields in which success is more difficult to achieve or in which the rewards come in less tangible forms. While some vocational workers try to help students to select careers that will provide intellectual and creative satisfactions as well as the material ones, the emphasis of most guidance people remains upon those fields that will lead to the greatest material rewards—or at the worst they will provide the student with job security and a safe future.

Some values stem directly from the concept of vocational guidance itself. Of these, the most basic center around the idea that facts plus self-knowledge make possible a reasoned vocational choice. In all vocational guidance, nothing is valued more highly than the reasoned vocational choice. And yet everything in experience, psychology, and education indicates that such a choice is impossible. Students choose their careers not on the basis of reasoning alone, but against the background of their experiences, feelings, concepts of self, and all the other components that go to make them the individuals they are. Enough has already been said about the "facts" and the items that supposedly contribute to self-knowledge to establish the fallacy inherent in the concept of a reasoned vocational choice. The fact that such a choice is one of the major values of the guidance field exerts a tremendous effect upon students and their parents. Students are expected and hence expect themselves to arrive at career decisions by a process of which they are incapable. Even if they were capable of this kind of reasoning it is unlikely that reasoning alone could help students to arrive at suitable and happy vocational decisions, for such a process omits not only the feelings of the individual but also the values inherent in any decision.

Second in the values inherent in vocational guidance is the idea of realism. The reasoned vocational decision must be a realistic one. The earlier discussion of realism raised the questions, Realistic according to whose value system and whose judgment, and realistic in terms of yesterday, today, or tomorrow? It suffices here to pose the hypothetical case of the student who, on the basis of "facts," self-knowledge, and reasoning, arrives at an "unrealistic decision." What then?

Last but not least among the values of vocational guidance is the one which views a vocational decision as final and unchangeable. Once the student has made his vocational decision on the basis of facts that are not facts, self-knowledge that is often fallacious or at best only half-knowledge, and reasoning that is a compound of thought, feeling, whim, impulse, prejudice, and many other elements, he learns that his choice is final, irrevocable, the end! Many students have come to look upon their early vocational decisions as strait jackets from which they cannot escape and which they dare not change.[2] The immutability of the vocational decision is a value which vocational guidance workers have transmitted to students thanks to their own lack of flexibility and comprehension of the values inherent in their approach to their work.

Reasoned decision, realism, and finality of choice are probably the three most important values in vocational guidance. In and of themselves, these values are neither good nor bad, but in their

---

[2] Professor Clay Gerkin, director of the Counseling Center at the University of Nebraska, has for several years studied the values of students at the University. Unfortunately, he has not prepared his findings for publication, but his continuing research constitutes one of the most interesting studies of student values done in any institution. One of his findings is that students themselves are increasingly holding in high esteem the person who knows what he wants to do and pursues this single definite goal. Once committed to a field of endeavor, the worst thing a student can do, according to the students, is change his mind. Changing is almost equivalent to admitting defeat or inadequacy.

application by many vocational guidance workers they have done immeasurable harm to many students who are either not ready to make a vocational choice or not willing to do so at a particular time. Why should students be required to make a vocational choice before they are allowed to graduate from high school? What does this requirement do to the student whose values will not permit him to fill in the blank with any old career that comes to his mind? What about the student who is regarded as odd because he has not yet decided where he is going and what he wants to do? And what about the student who reads in the Sunday paper the following advice: When able to do your job well, "ask for more responsibility in your company—or a different job. If you don't get it, get the hell out." [3] Since Mr. Lear has made his million, how are students to reconcile his advice with that of their guidance people especially since students, too, judge success according to current values?

[3] William P. Lear, "My Six Secrets Can Make You a Million Dollars," *This Week Magazine*, September 3, 1961, pp. 14–15.

Part III

IMPLICATIONS

THERE IS NO point in examining the myths of vocational guidance and the discernible actualities of the current scene unless implications for new and different approaches and practices result. Examination of myths is not enough; because they are traditional, myths will continue in operation until something new is offered to replace them. The voice of the critic, like that of the turtle, may be heard throughout the land, but will avail nothing if destruction alone is its purpose.

From a historical point of view, criticism of vocational guidance has always been a dangerous process. Faced with criticism, vocational guidance practitioners hasten to rationalize their traditional approaches and defensively cling to them even more completely. Such self-imposed ostrichism does not produce positive action. In a few instances the verbiage may change a little and the traditional may be masked with a new name, but mere verbal changes cause only additional confusion, not newness or modification. Rechristening is nothing more than a superficial salaam to new knowledge and developments.

The critic faces yet another problem. In modern education any suggestions for abolishing practices are too often dimissed as negative. Educational systems have developed by addition, not by the subtraction of what is outmoded or nontenable. Today the word negative is presumed to counter any criticism and to allow tradition to remain secure and unmolested. At times, however, the most positive approach is that of abolishing practices, regardless of vested interests and the forcefulness of myths.

Implications, therefore, take several forms: suggestions for the abolishing of certain beliefs and practices, recommendations for new methodologies, and the distinguishing of possible sound theories relating to man and work. These implications deal with the meaning of the myths and actualities, the resultant school program, and the counselor himself and his training.

Even inscribing an epitaph on the field of vocational guidance can be a positive action. Although modern medicine, for example, retains only the oath of Hippocrates, it grew because of the work of that man. So also vocational guidance furnishes the take-off point for the potential of the future. *Requiescat in pace* can be written with thankfulness and appreciation.

Chapter 10

THE MEANING OF IT ALL

Out of the myths of vocational guidance and the actualities of the modern world come some fundamental implications for the future of guidance work. These basic meanings are positive in nature, for they point directions. Even though they take the form of critical conclusions about vocational guidance, they incorporate possibilities for the future of counseling.

The time is past when school guidance workers can remain content with the *status quo* and find solace in time-worn excuses for a lack of an analytical and critical view. The cold war, Sputnik, and the tensions created by them have outlawed lethargy and apathy. Guidance cannot remain stagnating in tradition or it may not exist at all. It must meet modern needs, for its success or failure in doing so may determine the fate of the nation.

Unfortunately the entire area of vocational guidance has not been examined and synthesized in terms of school practices and reshaped to fit the actualities. The conclusions and possibilities analyzed here are and should be of concern to every person working, or interested, in school guidance.

Conclusions

The conclusions arising from myths strike at the basis of vocational guidance theory and practice. Although many schools no longer label their programs vocational, but have turned to the simpler term, guidance, these conclusions apply to all guidance programs. Not many new guidance practices have actually appeared in the schools since those first developed by vocational guidance practitioners. Any school guidance worker should look at the five conclusions with the old adage in mind, "If the shoe fits, put it on."

The first major conclusion is that *there is no sound theory underlying existing practices.* There are many speculations about theories both of vocational guidance and of individual choice of vocation, but none of these theories has influenced old-style practices. Any theoretical statement that does not affect what is being done obviously has no practicability. It is empty theorizing.

Vacuous theory usually exists when the theorists are using current practices as a starting point and establishing the theories to justify the practices. The process is a bit like viewing what is being done and then asking, Why are we doing it? Theory, to be adequate, must start with modern knowledge about human behavior, and practices consistent with that theory must then be developed. Otherwise the result is a cycle of endless confusion from which no new fundamental learnings or development accrue.

Perhaps no adequate modern theories of vocational guidance will ever be developed because *there is no justification for the separate practice of vocational guidance, or the more popular modern epithet, vocational counseling.* Vocational decisions and problems have too long been viewed as something discrete, separate from the individual as a whole. No individual makes any decision from a framework other than his total personality. In view of modern psychological theory, the separation of an individual's concerns into the popular categories of personal, social, educational, and vocational with a special counselor for each is not only a complete absurdity, but dangerous and destructive to the individual. Nevertheless, such fallacious division has continued for half a century despite modern discoveries concerning psychology and counseling. If the basis for both theory and practice is unsound, how can a valid theory be set forth?

The reasons for the continuance of such artificial categories are many, external, and unrelated to twentieth-century developments. School guidance workers appointed to their work without adequate counselor training seem to find security in an information-giving and -receiving role closely resembling that they filled as teachers. Other school guidance workers believe that they should not "meddle with personality" and hence feel less meddlesome freely giving vocational advice, little realizing that this act is the greatest meddling of all, for what a person does and becomes is a dynamic part of his personality. Still other guidance workers are caught in the lure of the myths. Nothing in their education has taught them to question the myths or even to view them as such. Everyone is doing it, why shouldn't they? Whatever the reason, the result is the same: the continuity of myths and the separation of vocational guidance into a distinct field, which it is not and never can be.

The third conclusion is that *all of vocational guidance rests upon an invalid assumption.* Research, experience, and modern theorizing all indicate that there is no such thing as a single, early, wise, intellectual vocational decision. Regardless of beginning theoretical changes, the assumption that there is continues to pervade the vocational guidance field and to control practices. In fact, the popularity of many of the totally useless practices stems from this basic misconception.

Analysis of the myths proves the inaccuracy of each of the words in the key phrase "a single, early, wise, intellectual vocational decision." Anyone honestly reviewing as many of his vocational choices as he can remember must admit that relatively few, if any, human beings make a single vocational choice. As a person matures, develops, and broadens his experiences, his interests change and his vocational decisions alter. His developmental pattern is an ever-expanding series of vocational decisions, for every choice he makes as a human being alters slightly what he does and, more often than not, the fields he enters. Hence decisions about occupations and employment reflect a gradual unfolding and changing of the self-concept and the needs that employment satisfies. Sometimes necessity limits the number of choices a person actually has, but it does not affect the basic pattern. It is strange that school counselors cling to and foster the time-worn myth of a single vocational decision when they themselves, by the mere act of becoming counselors, have made a fundamental shift in vocation, from teaching to counseling—two quite dissimilar kinds of work.

In like manner, the idea of forcing vocational choices early does nothing more than limit exploration and cause difficulties for the youngster involved. Any adult conversing with a youngster will sooner or later ask, "What do you want to be when you grow up?" Depending upon his interests at the moment, the child will answer candidly in terms of the occupations with which he is most familiar. By the age of ten or twelve, he finds that adults are no longer pleased or satisfied with his changing answers so he may protect himself by one of two devices: either he says honestly he does not know, or he repeats some answer that has already brought approval from his parents and other adults. Many are the proud parents who state with conviction that their sons and daughters plan to become engineers, lawyers, or doctors. The youngster is virtually stuck with his decision, made not wisely, intellectually, and knowingly, but rather on the basis of adult approval. It is no wonder that he views changing his mind as a mortal sin, for adults force him into this trap.

Perhaps the most interesting paradox connected with the idea of a single early vocational decision is that current vocational guidance practices try to parlay the idea in two ways. Vocational exploration is a continually parroted phrase at the same time that all the current practices serve to delimit exploration and to narrow choices into the early decision. Most teachers of courses in occupations judge the success of their teaching by the number of students who have made a single early choice—in fact, many teachers demand that youngsters state for them their top two or three choices of occupations in order to pass such a course. Most adults, caught in the tangles of the myth, hold in high esteem the youngster who knows what he wants to be, knows it early, and does not change his mind. These adults wear blinders that prevent them from seeing the modern world of actualities and the true nature of human personality.

Psychology has taught for half a century that man is not just an intellectual being, but the old divisions of faculty psychology separating man into his intellectual and emotional parts persist. Their effect on vocational guidance is seemingly unalterable. Man does not make an intellectual vocational decision or even decisions. He chooses his occupation in the same manner he chooses his wife or his latest automobile—through a blending of intellect, emotions, motivations, happenstance, needs, and all the adjustive defenses he uses to protect and enhance his self-concept. Until this *fact* is truly recognized in both education and counseling, no progress can or will be made. Similarly, no real amount of good and a great deal of harm will result unless the concept of a single, early, wise, intellectual vocational decision is interred with the bones of the outmoded psychology from which it sprang.

In 1957 the present authors examined guidance practices and asked for a thorough analysis of some of the untested assumptions on which current practices were predicated.[1] At that time we delineated six questionable assumptions that were unexamined, hallowed, and inviolate although only tradition seemed to lie behind them: (1) most, if not all, of the present guidance-personnel procedures and practices should be retained; (2) most guidance-personnel procedures are worthy of continuing refinement; (3) guidance-personnel work as it affects the majority of students can and should operate only on an informational level; (4) a complete and effective guidance-personnel program is one that incorporates most, if not all, of the current procedures; (5)

---

[1] Ruth Barry and Beverly Wolf, *Modern Issues in Guidance-Personnel Work* (New York, Bureau of Publications, Teachers College, Columbia University, 1957).

present procedures and practices implement present guidance-personnel aims; (6) guidance-personnel procedures and practices developed in the past are adequate to meet current needs. The questions we then raised about procedures and practices are as valid and significant today as they were in the spring of 1957, before Sputnik changed our view of the universe. Although many parts of *Modern Issues* have been hotly debated before the major associations, no discussions of the traditional practices have occurred. And yet there is nothing more fundamental to all aspects of guidance-personnel work than what the worker does to and for students day by day.

Somehow guidance practices never receive the analysis their questionable nature should produce. Recent developments may affect theory slightly, but not practices. Now, as in 1957, the same questions must be raised about guidance practices and procedures. In fact, an analysis of the myths connected with many of them produce the fourth major conclusion: *the most widely used guidance practices defeat rather than implement the aim of helping the student.*

In the typical school the guidance worker devotes the majority of his time to informational activities: the administration of tests, statistical analysis of the results, school-wide interpretation of the scores, procuring and filing occupational and educational information, dissemination of that information, planning for career and college nights, advisement of students about their school programs in ten- or fifteen-minute interviews, and the encouragement of a "realistic" career choice on the basis of all the available information. In many schools where the informational services are paramount and extensive, work with the student as an individual is often an accounting process.

Standardized tests are today the chief source of information about students. In both industry and educational institutions, tests are overused, rarely understood, and, more frequently than not, misinterpreted. Most efforts since the 1920's have been devoted to the refinement of the same basic types of objective instruments, preferably those that yield numerical results as if

statistics and numbers were sufficient to describe human personality. In the attempt to deal with test scores as though they were
absolutes, counselors and personnel officers tend to ignore mar-
gins of error and the questionable nature of many, if not all, tests.

Any good counselor must ask himself what the scores from
tests really mean in terms of concepts that are at best vaguely
understood, such as intelligence, aptitudes, and interests. He
must remember that statistical manipulation is a process for dealing with the scores of large groups of people and that, although
the current standardized tests may yield some information about
groups of students, they have less validity for the individual as
an individual. Yet tests and test scores are constantly used as
individual not group devices.

Nothing is more dangerous to the individual than the misinterpretation of test results. The counselor who has taken a course
or two in measurement may have some little understanding of the
weaknesses of the tests he administers, but usually he becomes
lost in the profile sheets and statistics and treats the scores as
though they were absolutes. The people with whom he works,
not having his background in measurement, carry misunderstanding even further. The result is, at best, confusion and, at worst,
irreparable damage to a person's self-concept. Unless all who deal
with tests understand completely their weaknesses as well as their
strengths, the tests should never be used.

The field of measurement has reached a transitional point.
The familiar types of objective tests have been subjected to a
quarter of a century or more of continuing refinement and have
probably progressed as far as they can. The limit of refinement
has undoubtedly been reached. If real advances are to be made
in measurement, psychometrists will have to turn to projective
and expressive techniques and other methods as yet undevel-
oped. Measurement cannot advance in a sound manner, however, without fuller and deeper understanding of human personality, its components and interrelationships, and adequate
theories of perception. Perhaps the healthiest development in
guidance might be the declaration of a moratorium on standard-

ized tests and a period of concentration on understanding personality and perception.

The implications from the discussion of classification systems are evident. The time spent in training counselors in the uses of formal classification systems for information is wasted and might better be devoted to increasing the counselor's knowledge of, for example, real counseling. All the current classification systems simply separate the students from the information and delimit their opportunities for exploration. None of the current systems is designed exclusively for school or student use. Here, too, further refinements are senseless effort, for systems must serve purposes and counselors have yet to decide what those purposes shall be.

Both associations and governmental bureaus have spent more money on the development of traditional and antiquated occupational information than on any other aspect of guidance. Information, too, has reached the point of absurdity. With change the only constant, and new occupations rapidly proliferating beyond man's imagination to comprehend, no school counselor can be an informational expert and he should not try to be one. The pamphlets, books, brochures, and statistics that flood his desk are out of date before they reach him. Whether and in what way students actually benefit from such generalized and often misleading information is not known. And yet many vocational guidance counselors bury themselves in information and operate an informational office rather than a counseling one. They become teachers rather than counselors or even guidance workers.

Perhaps today the greatest amount of harm is done through the stress on realism. Realism as it applies to all aspects of life and personality is the new modern myth and the embodiment of all the remnants of the early Puritan values. It serves as a justification for all the outmoded mythological practices and as a projection of the counselor's own personal values. The counselor caught up in the cult of the "realistic self-concept" can readily damn all the counselee's new ideas, all his creativity and imagination, even all his hopes and interests, by the single word "unrealistic," for according to modern values, youngsters must be taught to be practical. They must be induced to concentrate not on "life, liberty, and the pursuit of happiness," but rather on the good job with the ample fringe benefits, the status symbols, the security, and the middle-class values. In modern society the current heavy emphasis on realism operates to produce conformity and to delimit students.

The strangleholds of the myths of vocational guidance cannot and will not be broken until counselors recognize honestly that most of the current procedures defeat aims and do not serve students well in the modern world. Hence the fifth conclusion is that *today's actualities necessitate new views and new approaches.* The delimiting and restricting aspects of vocational guidance and methodological theory are not consonant with the present actualities.

Questionable, traditional methods cannot solve today's problems and paradoxes. With all parts of the world accessible within ever-shortening periods of time, there is great need for understanding of different cultures and individuals, at the same time that the increased rigidity of the social structure and schools works to reduce understanding and to emphasize objectivity and the group. With the forces of bigness, social isolation, mass testing, and impersonalism apparent in every area, there is greater need than ever before for individual freedom, recognition, and independence. The old informational type of vocational guidance serves only to negate freedom rather than to enhance it. There is also great need for full utilization of the abilities of all people, yet all the current trends in employment and vocational planning tend only to curtail the contributions of many groups. Most important, modern America will progress or fall as a result of the opportunities given to or taken by imaginative, creative, thinking people. Many of the concepts integral to vocational guidance restrict the very qualities most desired today. The nation needs flexibility and new ideas, but from the educational function that is supposedly designed to help the individual student there come only rigidity and the reinforcement of outmoded values and concepts.

Change is the only certainty of the modern world; and changes are so rapid and so unpredictable that it is impossible even to attempt to steer students into as yet unknown occupations, and foolhardy to guide them toward the old ones. At this point most students would be far better off with no guidance whatsoever than with the traditional practices carried out by vocational counselors.

Although the implications for traditional vocational guidance are not promising, recent developments in allied fields and glimmerings of new theories offer directions for progress in the future. Old-time vocational guidance may be outmoded, but out of the work done in that field in the past come some of the possibilities for new theories and practices in the future.

Possibilities

New approaches grow through the contributions of many people, and so it is with the views of man and his work. Each theorist tends to stress the facets of personality most important to him or those he feels have been misinterpreted by others. Hence one can accept and reject certain parts of various formulations. The dangers arise when counselors embrace so thoroughly one single approach to their work that they tend to ignore new developments or to forget that truth is usually found somewhere in a synthesis of the various extremes.

Today there is available much knowledge about human behavior that has yet to find a real place in guidance practice. Out of this recent knowledge, however, new approaches and practices can be applied so that guidance in the schools will be in terms of the modern era and not of the turn of the century.

A favorite pastime of psychologists has been their attempts to categorize and compartmentalize human beings. Borrowing techniques from such fields as medicine, psychologists seem to feel a need to separate out various types of behavior, diagnose them in terms of cause and severity, and treat them only after a full diagnosis has been made. This concept has crept into education and school counseling. Both educators and counselors seem to feel more secure being able to diagnose students through tests and to group them by a variety of labels: IQ classifications, underachievers and overachievers, academic and nonacademic, troubled or nontroubled, and a host of other either-or epithets. Rarely do these people consider what such labeling does to students, for the individual is overlooked whenever groupings serve the adult's need for security.

Categorization seems to be an integral part of American values, and the most popular classification is by occupation. Adults seem to feel more secure with their fellow men when they are able to use the pigeonholing concept of occupation and all that the mere naming of an occupation implies—amount of education, social status, working hours, manner of dress, size of income, and all the many mental associations that the mention of an occupation conjures up. It is no wonder that the adults serving as teachers, counselors, and parents attempt to find the same sort of security by applying the same technique with youngsters. When a student states a vocational choice, categorization of him is easier, particularly if the adult approves of the choice. The youngster who states that he is uncertain defies societal values, for he cannot be readily classified. Disapproval is the natural adult reaction.

The first principle basic to new theory is in essence a total view of human personality—a principle psychologists have been emphasizing unsuccessfully for years. A holistic approach means that educators and counselors will have to shed all their attempts at simple categorization and compartmentalization and look at the individual as an entity, for human personality has so many facets that it defies categorization.

Vocational counseling, for example, usually begins and ends with the areas of the person's interests and aptitudes. These are but minor parts of the total human being, and parts neither well known nor understood. Vocational counselors must keep in mind R. L. Thorndike's warning that we simply "don't know enough to guide a man into a specific career." [2] We know even less about the nature and nurture of interests, and practically nothing about the broader psychological aspects of work. Any approach other than a holistic one is today impossible.

The second principle that should underlie sound theory stresses the dynamic aspects of personality. Man is an ever-developing, ever-changing being just as is the society in which he lives. Theoretically, students of human behavior since Heraclitus have discussed the dynamic qualities of men, but practically the concept of dynamism is absent in vocational guidance. Until permanent unchanging elements can be found in man's personality, it is absurd to assume that they exist. All measurement instruments deal with man at a single point in time and cannot predict well where he will be at another time and place.

Within the past ten years, new views of man as dynamic offer great potentiality for a different approach to man and work. A. H. Maslow, for example, maintains that man is an ever-striving individual trying to fulfill certain physiological and psychological needs basic to his nature. Even though questions may be raised about Maslow's designation and ordering of needs, there is little doubt that this challenging theory offers a positive and logical approach to personality. It offers, furthermore, a new look at vocations.

Maslow's approach has many implications for the old questions, Why does man work? and What satisfactions does he seek and gain thereby? The obvious answers are that man works in order to satisfy certain basic needs similar to those of others but still idiosyncratic to himself. A person with a strong need for belongingness will try to satisfy that need through a kind of work that will furnish group membership. When this particular need has been satisfied, he will then and only then seek other kinds of satisfaction through his work. This new search may

[2] From interview in New York *Herald Tribune,* December 13, 1959.

not be fulfilled in his present occupation and he will either become bored or try to change fields. And so the process goes. Obviously the needs of the teen-ager may not be the same as those he will feel as a man of thirty, forty, or sixty. Hence occupational satisfactions must be viewed as progressive and subject to acute changes.

In the same manner, interests change and develop. The little boy who stated firmly that he now knew more about pelicans than he cared to know was acknowledging a shift in interests. The teen-ager who suddenly becomes intrigued with taking apart and reassembling his automobile may be engaging in a transitory interest which he satisfies and then drops. Few people as adults are interested in the same things that fascinated them as children or even in the same pursuits from year to year. Interests, like needs, can and do enlarge and diminish, come into being and pass away.

One facet of dynamic personality that tends to be ignored is intelligence and the possible drives that this quality alone engenders within the person. Gradually many theorists are arriving at the conclusion that the interests of highly gifted and creative people are more varied and less subject to stabilization than those of less richly endowed persons. Today, however, vocational guidance practitioners tend to focus on the gifted and the creative in terms of having them concentrate on their early interests, make early vocational decisions, and pursue definite careers. Perhaps more harm is being done to the creative personalities in our society than to any other single group.

The only concept of work consonant with a dynamic theory of personality sees that endeavor as an expression of man's self in what he does. Hence *the third principle is that a man's work is an integral part of his self-concept.*[3] Through his work and his identification with it, a person either complements and enhances his picture of himself and his capabilities or he distorts it.

[3] Donald Super has done some excellent beginning theorizing along this line. See, for example, *Psychology of Careers* (New York, Harper, 1957).

No constructive approaches to job satisfaction will be forthcoming until they are expressed in terms of the person's needs, motivations, and self-concept. Certainly job satisfaction occurs only when a person's work and occupation meet his present needs and allow him to view himself as a worker in a way that matches his own concept of himself. In many cases a man's occupation becomes the focal point of his own identification: that is, he thinks of himself in terms of the work he does. Dissatisfaction results when others do not think of him in the same terms or when his own image of himself is greatly at variance with his current occupation. The person working as a clerk by day and a writer by night may think of himself primarily as a writer, whether or not he has any publications. Difficulties ensue when his friends view him as a clerk, or during the time when his employment forces him to think of himself in that role. Work and identification must match a person's self-concept if that person is to be happy and satisfied.

An overused phrase in vocational guidance today is "realistic self-concept." [4] The basic questions must be continually asked about this phrase, Realistic from whose point of view? Realistic at what point in time? The self-concept is not static. Like the personality which it shapes, self-concept is constantly altering, developing, and changing. Hence the job that melds with the self-concept at one point in time may neither meet needs nor "jibe" with a person's self-concept at another. Vocational choices, therefore, must be an on-going process and cannot be stabilized at a single point in time.

The fourth principle is that cultural values and expectations shape job choices in any society at any time. The culture quite literally produces the types of citizens it values. In like manner, vocational guidance practitioners inflict their interpretation and understanding of societal and personal values upon the students whom they advise. The dangers in this type of practice are readily apparent.

[4] See Chapter V, pp. 93–96.

The American culture is pluralistic. The values the counselor holds are seldom those of the students with whom he works. Similarly, the measurement instruments the counselor uses often reflect the values of the testmaker and the type of individual whom he respects and wishes to produce and perpetuate. Rare, however, is the study that even mentions the role values play in work and guidance.

Perhaps no true understanding of vocational choices and work can take place without thorough investigation of the varying value systems that influence the individual and society. A person's attitudes are a gradual development from his own experiences and the immediate and broad culture in which he lives. These values can be understood only in terms of the individual and the culture, and here lies the opportunity really to implement the concept of individual differences, for no counselor can function as a counselor without a willingness to accept not only measurable individual differences but also the fundamental differences in values.

Examples of how prominent value systems are in occupational choices are numerous from cultural anthropology and from historical studies. One culture values one type of citizen, another culture a different type. One era even in Western civilization produces a proliferation of Renaissance men or great musicians or philosophers or scientists. No counselor today should attempt to work in the vocational area without knowledge of cultures and societies. Seemingly, however, vocational guidance workers have ignored to date the cultural aspects of work and personality.

The fifth principle basic to all effective guidance is the old one of individual differences. Much lip service is paid to this principle, but practically no practices find their roots in it. In fact, practically none of the most popular guidance practices are devoted to the individual at all, but rather focus upon the group. A common procedure within the schools is for the counselor to see all students for a set amount of time at regular intervals. Similar standards are set for all students, and in many cases all students are expected to make vocational choices at the same time. Extra help for an individual student is usually offered only when that student differs so widely from the group that he cannot be tolerated. Then he is recognized as an individual, but only until he can become a conforming anonymous member of the group again. Guidance is and always has been a group, not an individual, endeavor.

An effective guidance program, however, must be built upon this fifth principle, for it offers real possibilities to meet the needs of the future. Many observers of the current scene deplore the loss of individuality within society and their fears are not empty or overly pessimistic. All present trends indicate that individuality will be even more at a premium within the next few decades when the forces of bigness and impersonalism really come to the fore. Guidance can then operate as an implement either to reduce individuality further and to reinforce conformity, or to release the creative power of the individual. Guidance workers must realize, however, which of their practices are focused upon the group and which offer potentialities for a real recognition of individual differences.

Psychological learnings must also be applied individually. Popular concepts such as developmental tasks are expressions of "the average." Not all students progress or mature at the same rate. In fact, today no one is certain whether the normal developmental tasks apply in any way to such special groups of students as the highly gifted and creative. Much more understanding is needed even of groups of people before a real start can be made toward recognition of the individual.

The last principle is as important for education as for guidance: *external learnings are relatively unimportant compared with internal learnings.* What is and becomes an integral part of each person influences directly what that person is and does. Such learnings do not take place overnight nor are they produced by external, informational means. Yet most current guidance practices do not operate at other than an information-giving or -receiving level. Nor do many educational methods. In the total picture of human personality, superficial information per se is perhaps the least important ingredient.

These six principles—a holistic approach, a concept of personality as dynamic, the importance of the self-concept, an understanding of values, a recognition of differences, and learning as internalization—offer the only possibilities for effective guidance in the future. Balanced against the conclusions derived from an analysis of myths and actualities, they signify only the long overdue end of traditional vocational guidance. This, in essence, is the meaning of it all.

Chapter 11

THE SCHOOL PROGRAM

ANY SUCCESSFUL program has two qualities, soundness and consistency. If the basic theory underlying a program is unsound, as in methodological vocational guidance, even consistent practices cannot compensate for its fundamental weakness. In like manner, a program may have modern aims that cannot be fulfilled because the procedures are totally inconsistent with these aims. Lack of the second quality is perhaps more insidious, for its nature deceives not only the lay public but the people working within it.

Unfortunately, most guidance programs today are missing one or the other of these two attributes. It is no wonder that there are so few real evaluative studies in the area. In the consistent but unsound program, evaluators start with a false premise. In the theoretically new but practically old, inconsistent programs, there can be no criteria to guide the evaluator. At times, guidance workers resemble a group of circus elephants parading around the ring in a tight circle with tails and trunks firmly locked, ignoring their surroundings and getting nowhere.

Today there is no excuse for unsound and inconsistent programs. The potentialities for sound theory and logical practices are present. What is needed is a policy to guide practices and a critical attitude toward what is now being done. Perhaps guidance workers need most of all a lack of fear and an infusion of imagination when they look at their own policy and practices.

Policy

Policy is simply a guide, a set of statements that furnish the index to the types of procedures needed and offer the criteria by which those practices may be evaluated. Each counselor in each school must set up his own statements of policy, for the special needs of each institution differ slightly. The basic policy statements contained in this chapter are necessarily general, but they serve to indicate an approach to the study of practices and to suggest the kinds of activities that are logically consistent with modern theory.

Within the past five or ten years, statements of policy for guidance programs have expanded in direct ratio to the number of guidance committees established and the number of job analyses of counselors put out by the schools. Guidance workers tend to think of all the high-sounding aims possible and to incorporate them into school policy, often with the tacit aim of extracting extra money from the school board to support such a noble endeavor. Seemingly the more aims included, whether consistent or not, the greater the possibility for cash. Often the counselor's task becomes so completely one of moving mountains that only Winston Churchill's comment could describe him in his work, "There but for the grace of God, goes God."

School policy statements should deal not only with the modern aims of the program but also simply and concretely with the day-by-day practices that need clarification. An excellent example is the area of confidentiality. Careful policy covering who communicates with whom, what types of information should be available or unavailable to school staff members and students, and who handles referrals can iron out many difficulties in advance. Clear policy makes the job of everyone in a school easier, for everyone knows and understands what is going on.

As a general approach to a modern school guidance program, the six principles outlined in the previous chapter can serve as a starting point for policy. Hence the first policy statement is that *the program should be dedicated primarily to serving the student,* not the counselor or the administration. An examination of the myths indicates how often practices are carried out to meet counselor needs for accomplishment and expertness, rather than student needs for self-knowledge and self-expression.

The second statement is equally simple: *the program must start with a holistic approach to human personality.* A counselor counsels people, not numerical scores from tests or the vocational or educational problems people presumably have. Counselors cannot split their duties by kinds of problems or by areas of concern, for these are usually the counselor's not the student's.

The traditional division of counselor duties may make paper administration of the program easier, but works to the detriment of the students involved. It also, at times, doubles the duties of guidance workers, for one student may be endlessly caught in a cycle of referrals from one special counselor to another.

Many vocational guidance leaders are today concerned about the approaches and practices used in the name of vocational guidance. Gradually the difficulties faced by researchers working on the Career Pattern Study are highlighting the many areas of weakness in vocational guidance. In a 1961 article, Donald Super deplores, "It may seem absurd that, with the vocational guidance movement more than 50 years old, we have found it necessary to devote more than six months to the definition of exploratory vocational behavior, but such is the case. . . ." [1] Despite the many weaknesses modern theorists find in vocational guidance, they seem unable to question the most fundamental of these shortcomings, the lack of a holistic view and a sound theory of personality, and try to make their suggestions within a vocational framework. The substitution of the phrase "vocational development" will neither remedy the weaknesses of old

[1] "Vocational Development, A Symposium," *The Personnel and Guidance Journal,* XL:14, September 1961. The three articles comprising this symposium are all interesting in that they call for a new stress on vocational development and do so chiefly in terms of pattern theory. They serve as an example of how the word vocational can limit possibilities for truly new concepts even among forward-thinking theorists.

vocational guidance concepts nor indicate new areas of practice. It may help to undermine some of the worst of the old practices, but these newer approaches will continue to be restricted by the fallacy of the vocational designation.

The third statement of policy is that *the program must serve to broaden the interests, experiences, learnings, and aspirations of students.* Most of the current popular practices have a specious quality that permits them to remain in operation even though fundamentally they are antithetical to the purpose of broadening. Indeed, it is a sorry comment on any endeavor to suggest that many of the most delimiting practices have continued because practitioners see nothing to substitute for them. A program, however, cannot be effective and will be detrimental without this third policy statement.

For decades, guidance workers have maintained that they have been adapting practices to particular schools, age groups, communities, and individuals. Nevertheless, the history of guidance belies the veracity of these claims, as do present-day programs. Practically never in the entire development of guidance has the fourth policy statement been implemented—that is, *the program must not be judged effective by its "completeness," but rather by how well it meets the particular needs of the students it serves.* Completeness is usually equated with the number of services proffered.

From its beginning, school guidance has been imitative, as has all education in this country. Perhaps imitation is an inevitable concomitant of a mass system of education but this point is difficult to judge because rarely has an alternative method appeared. Today, for example, accrediting agencies evaluate guidance programs on the number of varying services offered and the completeness of carefully filed occupational information; more often than not, the same numbers and kinds of tests are administered to students in schools of 40 as in schools of 5000, apparently on the assumption that the greater the number of tests, the better the program. Even supposedly modern recommendations for guidance programs, such as those of James B. Conant, equate the

quantity of services with the values of them and stress completeness as the greatest good. The number of services offered is no
index to quality—in fact, proliferation of services often has the
opposite effect of reducing quality when most of those services
are founded only on myths.

Similarly, there have been few attempts to adapt practices to
various age groups or individuals. The guidance services offered
to adults through U. S. Employment Agencies, Vocational Rehabilitation Agencies, and Vocational Counseling centers are
identical to those furnished for high school and even junior high
school students. The attempts at elementary school guidance in
New York City, for example, and the recommendations for such
guidance in textbooks on the subject demonstrate clearly the
repetition of the same practices with the young child. In New
York, vocational orientation begins in the third grade. Were
there not child labor laws, perhaps placement services might be
offered! This nonadaptive repetitiveness continues despite the
preliminary findings of the Career Pattern Study, which suggest
that most of the vocational guidance practices are *not* adaptable
even to high school students. Counselors today must drop the
concepts of quantitative completeness and imitation.

The fifth policy statement is that *what is done for one need
not be done for all*. A false notion of democracy and egalitarian-
ism seems to promote the idea that guidance services must be
doled out to all students in equal amounts. If a counselor sees
one student, he must see all students. Working on this premise,
many counselors engage in the patently absurd practice of
scheduling one or two fifteen-minute interviews with each student, even though the number may reach five hundred or a
thousand or even more. Such wholesale brief interviewing ac-
complishes nothing more than easing the counselor's mind
about the fairness of his policies. Actually it is a total waste of
time.

Not all students need the same amount of counseling; some
may not need counseling at all! Not all students need to take

the same kinds or numbers of tests at the same times. Not all students need guidance classes or information or any of the other group services justified in the name of vocational guidance. A program cannot help the individual by ignoring him in a concentration on the group.

The sixth policy statement is that *the program must be professional.* An adequate program cannot be run by a teacher suddenly designated a counselor or by a person untrained or only slightly trained for the work. Counseling of any type demands such skills that the students are better off with no guidance than with that foisted upon them by nonprofessional personnel.

Each counselor must, of course, supplement these six basic policy statements with others pertinent to his own situation. These six, however, supply a backdrop for the examination of current and possible practices.

The Practices

Fifty years ago there were literally no practices by which a counselor might have implemented the policy outlined in this chapter. Today there are still relatively few, for such policy outlaws most, if not all, informational services in the form and with the purposes they now have. External practices cannot function at an internal level and the aims of modern guidance must be internal or it has no *raison d'être*.

Within the past two decades a new middle ground of school counseling has come to the fore. Previously a counselor had no solid basis of either counseling theory or techniques to aid him in his work. Rather he had only the choice between the psychoanalytic methods designed for the abnormal personality or the age-old teaching methods of telling and advisement. Obviously neither set of techniques could serve him adequately in his work in helping normal youngsters to internalize behavioral learnings. Afraid of encroaching on psychoanalytic and therapeutic areas, the school counselor tended to run away from anything of a personal nature in his work with youngsters and to adhere strongly to the methods that had served him in the classroom from which he was usually recruited. Hence most school counselors were and remained advisers, using suggestion, scientific intepretation of test results, or "expertise" in all the peripheral areas like occupational information and study habits.

Today the school counselor no longer faces such a Hobson's choice. New counseling techniques growing out of psychological counseling and readily adaptable to school counseling are available. Perhaps more of modern counseling might have penetrated school guidance had not the new developments seemed to threaten the half-century-old advisement practices to such an extent that guidance workers effectively blocked such advances by the red herring of a directive versus nondirective controversy. At present that controversy should be buried, for the new type of counseling that has arisen from the work of the misnamed nondirective therapists and counselors offers the possibility for real counseling within the schools.

Modern counseling starts with the premise that the youngster with professional help can develop enough self-understanding to enable him to solve his own problems and make his own decisions. Essentially such counseling is a process of internalized learning that allows the student to explore his own feelings, motivations, and experiences and relate them to his behavior. Only by this method of internalization can a youngster come to decisions for himself about himself. In contrast, advisement allows the counselor to attempt to shape the student's life. With the implements now available to the adviser, such a process is faulty at best and extremely dangerous at worst. There is simply no rationale on the basis of which an adviser can attempt to play God and suggest or dictate decisions to a student. And yet, everyday thousands of advisers in schools all over the country tell students what to do and mislabel their work, counseling.

The purpose of this book is not to outline modern counseling methods.[2] Rather it is sufficient to point out that training in modern counseling is now available and that such counseling must lie at the core of any effective guidance program. There are no possible substitutes, for counseling alone operates on other than a mythological informational level. Full formal acceptance of this approach came in March 1961, when the Joint Commission on Mental Illness and Health, made up of professional representatives from medicine, psychology, and allied fields, recommended that such be the province of the school counselor.[3] Unfortunately, this important statement has not received the attention it warrants, for so far there has been little apparent impact upon school guidance programs.

There are no short cuts to effective counseling. Rigidity in administrative policy combined with misuse of counselors makes many programs inoperable, for too often the counselor tends to be ineffective because of the great number of students he is expected to see or the restrictions limiting his work to those demonstrating the most aberrant behavior. Both procedures are fallacious. Summers of experimental work in counseling with groups of highly gifted students [4] have, for example, proved the value and validity of counseling with this group on a voluntary basis. Most of these students, in fact, made their own distinctions be-

---

[2] For a full explanation of all aspects of school counseling see Ruth Barry and Beverly Wolf, *Developmental School Counseling*, to be published by the Bureau of Publications, Teachers College, Columbia University. A recent book with a similar approach is that by Dugald Arbuckle, *Counseling: An Introduction* (Boston, Allyn & Bacon, 1961).

[3] The text of the statement should be required reading for all school counselors. The brief recommendation states that, "nonmedical mental health workers with aptitude, sound training, practical experience and demonstrable competence should be permitted to do general, short-term psychotherapy. . . ." The report defines this as "the treating of persons by objective, permissive, nondirective techniques of listening to their troubles and helping them resolve their troubles. . . ."

[4] The counseling work being carried on at the University of South Dakota with groups of students gifted in science, mathematics, speech, and dramatics will be summarized when follow-up studies are completed.

tween what counseling accomplished and what they were unable to obtain from what they termed "guidance." They equated guidance with test interpretation and advisement. True counseling takes time, but students recognize and appreciate the difference between it and guidance. If a school system does not have a sufficient number of trained counselors, the solution to its dilemma is not to be found in group practices or in the use of nonprofessional personnel, but rather lies in acknowledging limitations and training more counselors for the schools. Any other solution is basically dishonest.

Counseling not only comprises the heart of the program but also supplies the focus for other procedures, for if modern counseling is consistent with the policy outlined, no procedures can be inconsistent with counseling. Hence examination of popular practices must be done in the light of both policy and counseling.

No practice today is more time-consuming for the school counselor than the administration, statistical analysis, recording of scores, and interpretation of standardized tests. Practically every school staff member and the students themselves wonder, What is the value of such extensive measurement and what part should it play in a school counseling—not guidance—program?

Today, unfortunately, no school can afford not to test its students. So long as test scores determine college admission and often employment, no student should miss the practice of taking standardized tests. Practice plays a great part in test results, for the student who has taken innumerable tests tends to be able to perform better on them than the student without this advantage. Questions are similar; vocabulary items are duplicated; practice in thinking in analogies helps. Unless and until sounder methods are found for distinguishing among people, or all institutions declare a moratorium on objective measurement, objective testing has to be done in the schools.

Perhaps it might be fairer and more honest if practice were the acknowledged aim of school testing programs. Certainly the way the test results are now being used, they have absolutely no counseling purpose. At least such honesty would not lead the school staff members or the students into misconceptions about what tests indicate or about the part they play in the counseling program. Tests might under these circumstances be used with less threat and personal involvement. Being honest about the purpose of measurement might also insure that school personnel would select the best tests available, not just the cheapest or the easiest to score, for the best tests offer the best practice for the students.

Achievement tests, for example, might serve several purposes, but not in the way they are now being used. They are excellent for practice largely because they differ in subject matter covered. Achievement tests can also serve in the diagnosis of educational and teaching weaknesses and strengths. This purpose, however, can be accomplished only by using the actual tests and not simply the test scores. If the tests are worth giving at all, they are worth the time spent in going over the questions with the students. Achievement batteries are educational devices and should be viewed as such.

Tests of intelligence or scholastic aptitude can serve a counseling purpose, but again not in the way in which they are presently used. Every school counselor should be trained to use such individual intelligence tests as the Stanford-Binet and the Wechsler-Bellevue for both children and adults. These tests, however, should not be administered to the entire student body. Rather the counselor should use them as counseling devices, for often they serve as excellent starting points for or supplements to the counseling process. Unfortunately, when a counselor uses these individual tests, he frequently does so with the sole object of obtaining a definite numerical score—not with the purpose of counseling the student in mind.

Interest and personality inventories should never be given to all students. Not only are they a waste of school time and money but they defeat the policies set up for modern guidance programs. Interest inventories delimit at the very time that broadening of student interests should be the goal. Personality inventories have so many weaknesses that they create more problems than they solve. Any well-trained counselor can learn far more about students through one good counseling session than he can through all the interest and personality inventories he might administer.

Aptitude testing, if done at all, should be handled cautiously and the results viewed with considerable skepticism. In the light of Thorndike and Hagen's study,[5] aptitude test scores should not be used directly for educational or career planning. The experience of taking an aptitude battery may, however, help the student in his attempt to gain self-understanding and to examine his interests and capabilities. In this process, of course, the scores are totally unimportant.

Perhaps the chief difficulty with using measurement in a modern program is not only confusion about the purposes, but also the counselor's own misconception of his role in relation to tests. Given a test score, most counselors lay aside their counseling role and become teachers, advisers, and statisticians. They try to teach students the meaning of measurement in one or two simple (or not so simple) lectures and then tell them numerical scores as though they were absolutes. The effect of this approach on students is hard to predict. One talented youngster, for example, was distressed because he scored at the 98th percentile on an achievement test. He had carefully figured out the total number of people who were "brighter" than he! Despite their training in measurement, counselors when given their own test scores will react precisely as this student did. In dealing with measurement, the counselor must remember that he is a counselor, otherwise his use of tests will defeat not implement the policies set up for his program.

The second most time-consuming practice in most schools is information and the collecting and disseminating of it. Guidance workers collect vast amounts of data about students and organize complete cumulative records. Teachers are expected to make

---

[5] Robert L. Thorndike and Elizabeth Hagen, *Ten Thousand Careers* (New York, John Wiley, 1959).

comments and these, too, become a part of the student's file. Usually these comments are simply value judgments about the students, such as "Good student," "Works hard," or "Pleasant personality," and tell more about the likes and dislikes of the teachers than they do about the individual students. If even half the time spent in refining cumulative records and in collecting relatively useless information were devoted either to an analysis of the uses of records or to the development of new practices, counseling might make some real headway in the schools.

The second aspect of information was discussed in Myths, Part I of this book. The reverence for well-kept files and "factual, authentic" information has reached absurd proportions. Information is a teaching device. It is only reasonable to assume that teachers working in their areas of expertness can know more about types of work in those areas than can counselors. Counselors have other important functions, and any teacher not interested enough in his own field to know something about educational and career opportunities in it is not fulfilling his teaching function. Information should be up-to-date and freely available to the students in the classrooms, library, and study halls. The teaching function, of course, includes helping the students to evaluate informational materials for themselves.

Information obtainable in the library or the counselor's office only on request of the student defeats the policy outlined. Such a method presumes that the student has enough knowledge to ask for particular information, whereas browsing through information should supply a broadening of the student's vistas. Furthermore, information should deal with the unusual, for most students are all too familiar with the usual. In most schools in the country today, information could be made to serve the students far better than it does.

There is another subtle difficulty involved in informational programs. The amount and type of information a school possesses and makes available to its students can in itself be limiting. A collection of college catalogues, for example, must be complete or students will make their selections of colleges on the basis of incomplete data already subjected to the selective process of the counselor. Similarly, the counselor himself will tend to suggest those colleges about which he knows something and discourage students from applying to those he does not know. Most files of college catalogues in schools are far from complete and contain only information about the local colleges or those the students from that particular high school tend to select. Counselors justify their omissions by the rationalization that their students are not interested in other colleges—seemingly never questioning whether the lack of interest might be a result of the counselor's point of view and the available materials. Sometimes incomplete information is far worse than no information at all.

Even those counselors who question information in general, cling tenaciously to two pet procedures dating from early vocational guidance: the community survey and career days or nights. Both serve a purpose but that purpose is not one of counseling or guidance, but public relations. Viewed objectively, the community survey of occupations is impossible in a large city, unnecessary in a small town, and usually incomplete even in a medium-sized city. It does more to acquaint business and industrial personnel with the fact that the school has some sort of guidance than it does to teach the students anything about a broad range of occupations. In like manner, the big career day or night serves no counseling or even informational purpose for the students, but it often impresses the community with what the counselor himself is trying to do and with the existence of a guidance program. As a personal public relations device for the counselor it is excellent, but the counselor should not deceive himself or the public into believing that such practices have anything to do with counseling or the effectiveness of his program. Once again, the counselor must be honest about the purpose of his practices and the policies they implement, for he has no other means by which to evaluate his efforts.

Group guidance practices of all types have enjoyed unprecedented popularity during the past few years and present trends indicate that this popularity will increase as more students flock into the schools. Most group guidance classes are rightly named classes, for all the paraphernalia that educators consider necessary classroom adjuncts are a part of them—syllabi, assignments, tests, grades, and lectures. Any resemblance to counseling or counseling aims is purely accidental. No one has asked the basic question, Is it possible to teach self-understanding by conventional methods? For that matter, Is it possible to *teach* motivation, understanding of feelings, societal values, courage, or any of the other internalized abstractions by informational courses labeled Justice 202 or Valor 191? Sometimes small groups of students led by a counselor with specialized training in group counseling (not in group dynamics or a single course in group information) can fulfill real counseling aims. These groups, however, must be select and all participants must share common problems. All of the current group practices need careful re-examination in terms of what they do to individual students before they are continued in modern guidance programs.

One of the most common guidance gimmicks today is the homeroom period of ten or fifteen minutes that begins the school day in many institutions. During these periods announcements are read, elections are held, roll is taken, excuses are heard, money is collected, and the business of the school is conducted. If such activities are neecssary for the efficient running of the school they must be carried out, but they serve an administrative not a counseling purpose. In theory the homeroom period may serve to afford the opportunity for some guidance activities, but in practice it seldom does. The counselor who wants a truly effective program must not fool himself into believing that the homeroom will contribute to it.

Only clear analysis of practices in terms of their aims and accomplishments can help the counselor to divorce worth-while from useless or misleading procedures. The alternative, when he finds that a traditional practice does not implement his aims or his policy, is to eliminate the practice, or at least relegate it to its proper position in his hierarchy of activities. If this approach were carried out, the counselor would have time for counseling and for research and experimentation with new types of practices. The modern counselor has an obligation to try to improve his work and he cannot wait for improvement to come from someone else. New theoretical formulations and research on methods are not the exclusive province of university research centers or individual college professors. Each counselor must himself have the ability to evaluate what is best for the school and the community in which he works. Without such individual effort there is no healthy future for guidance and counseling.

The Starting Point

One common question is, At what point should guidance be offered in the schools? Where should it start? Increasingly counselors are answering, The earlier the better. This question, however, does not really hit at the heart of the matter, because the starting point for school counseling depends upon several questions in addition to the superficial one of time—What form should it take? Who should do it? What purposes should it serve?

If, in thinking of guidance, one visualizes the traditional vocational guidance program, there is obviously no need for it in the elementary schools—in fact, there is no need for it at any educational level. If, however, one thinks in terms of modern counseling, there is great need for it in the lower grades. Difficulties, learnings, and motivations are cumulative and no adage is truer in psychology than that "It is easier to help a person to understand his behavior and alter it, if it needs altering, before patterns have been firmly set." Real counseling work with youngsters is neither extensive nor well-known, but counselors must concentrate upon adapting methods from their work with teen-agers and adults and from play therapy to counseling with elementary school children. Until such adaptations are made there is no use in discussing elementary school guidance, for there is no point in repeating the mistakes of the past in a new setting.

Many books on the market preach one message: guidance through the classroom teacher. Naturally the classroom teacher must be familiar with new developments in learning theory and methods and educational psychology as they apply to the classroom if he is to be the most effective teacher possible. However, a teacher functioning as a teacher is not a counselor. Teachers have neither the time nor the training to cope with youngsters' feelings, motivations, fears, and self-doubts. A teacher is trained as a teacher and that is his only role unless and until he becomes professionally trained as a counselor.

Nothing has caused more disgruntlement than the popular practice of in-service training for teachers to enable them to function as members of a guidance team. Such short-term courses usually offered by the school counselor cover briefly all the traditional aspects of guidance work. Many school guidance workers expect the teachers after a short in-service course to perform such functions as interviewing with students, interpreting tests to them, and teaching group guidance classes. In many schools a ridiculous situation results. The unqualified teachers are doing whatever personal contact work with students takes place and the counselor is sitting in his office coping with information and statistics! No wonder many teachers object to participating in a guidance program. No one feels secure or adequate working outside his area of competence. Regardless of how many more students can be reached by this approach, reaching students is not equivalent to helping them. If teachers are to assist in guidance, their assistance should be in their area of competence, the dissemination of information. Only a trained counselor should do the counseling either with individuals or with small groups of students.

The third question, What purposes should a counseling program serve? lies at the base of much recent controversy about the schools. Many critics have maintained that guidance and especially group guidance or social adjustment classes are fads and frills that should have no part in an educational program, and that they are a waste of time and money. When these critics speak of traditional guidance practices they are right. The danger in their charges, however, is that in sweeping out the traditional and outmoded, they tend also to eliminate the valuable, where it exists.

Modern counseling serves a definite educational purpose, that of learning, and there is no other sound purpose for schools. Only the student who learns to cope with his own problems, who can realize his own abilities, who can establish his own motivations, and who can seek his own goals will receive full benefit from the educational experience at the same time that he is helped to profit from other such experiences.

Perhaps traditional guidance programs will continue until educators themselves honestly review the purposes of educational institutions and decide what these purposes are. Decisions about purposes must answer another basic question, What can the schools do best that no other social institution can do? Only by answering this question can educators separate the fads and frills of traditional vocational guidance from the truly educational aspects of counseling.

Chapter 12

THE COUNSELOR

THE FOREGOING analysis of vocational guidance has implications not only for the field in general and for school programs but also for the counselor who will carry on the work and observe its effectiveness or lack thereof with the students. Many school guidance people have for a long time been the foremost critics of the traditional approach to vocational guidance and have been asking for some more workable substitute. Unfortunately their comments and criticisms seldom appear in the journals or on convention programs, so that the undercurrent of unrest and dissatisfaction among workers in the schools has been easily ignored.

The myths and actualities of vocational guidance have implications for the focus of the counselor's work, the training that enables him to carry on his work, the values that he holds, and the kind of person he is and will become. In all these areas vocational guidance workers need help in clarifying their ideas and in rethinking their purposes and how their programs implement those purposes. Workers need, too, to develop a perspective that can allow them to assign to the vocational aspects of the work a position in school programs appropriate to their limited importance.

Focus

The first guidance program in the schools began with the expressed purpose of selecting students for the overcrowded vocational high schools in Boston. Presumably the major focus was upon the selection process, but the problem of which students might profit from and contribute to the vocational schools entered too. Probable vocational choice also influenced this initial guidance program, for it determined the high school and the program of each individual student. Focus in this program was neither clear-cut nor definite, but included such diverse, and sometimes conflicting, elements as selection, early vocational choice, educational planning, and the "good" of the individual student.[1]

As the guidance movement got under way in the schools, the focus narrowed to the vocational aspects of students and student planning, with secondary attention to educational planning as it contributed to the vocational. Much of this narrowing was implicit rather than explicit. Vocational workers would tell a questioner that their greatest concern was for the student as a person, but a careful examination of their programs would reveal that the focus, if it was directed toward the student at all, was upon the student as a potential worker. Much the same situation existed within the training programs, where trainers would claim a focus upon the student, but, in their emphases, course offerings, and teaching methods, the focus they implemented might be upon anything from testing to occupational information to administration.

The problems of indefinite focus, multiple focuses, and undetermined focus still plague school guidance workers. Thanks to the lack of focus within the guidance area as a whole and the many possible focuses within the specialized area of vocational guidance, the program within any particular school is usually centered upon whatever the counselor in charge considers to be his area of strength. If the counselor finds testing especially interesting and feels secure in it, his program is likely

---

[1] For an earlier discussion of focus and some of the other points in this chapter, see Ruth Barry and Beverly Wolf, *Modern Issues in Guidance-Personnel Work* (New York, Bureau of Publications, Teachers College, Columbia University, 1957).

to focus upon measurement and profile sheets. If the counselor prefers information, his focus may be on brochures, career days, and filing systems. Despite a long history of protestations to the contrary, guidance people have never been able to develop, maintain, and implement a focus upon the student in all of his many aspects. And yet it is precisely this emphasis upon the individual student and his problems of growing up in a complex society that is needed today. The focus in guidance should be where it has never been—upon the student.

Only in the guidance programs which emphasize counseling is there a beginning of truly active concentration upon the individual student. Even within some counseling programs, however, the focus upon the individual gets lost in a morass of other emphases. Anyone who has listened to the bitter, disillusioning experiences of some veterans consulting Veterans Administration vocational "counselors" knows that the focus there was only theoretically upon counseling and actually upon measurement, diagnosis, advisement, and coercion, with the individual's desires and feelings in many instances receiving little or no attention. Even in modern counseling, some counselors have found it difficult, if not impossible, to sort out and maintain a consistent focus upon the individual largely because there are so many inconsistencies and misunderstandings about focus among guidance practitioners.

It is odd that guidance workers seem to find focus troubling, because it is not a difficult concept to understand and should lend itself to easy definition by people professing interest in other people. For guidance workers, and more especially for anyone who aspires to the title of counselor, the only possible focus is upon the individual student. This definition of focus will enable the guidance worker to deal constructively with the myths of vocational guidance, for it will enable him to answer without hesitation the questions, Which is more important, the test or the student? The occupational pamphlet or the student? The filing system or the student? The realistic vocational choice or the student?

All too often programs are diffuse, tangential, and superficial simply because guidance workers have no definite idea of what their primary concern should be. If they knew where they should direct their attention, they could establish programs that would have consistency, direction, and purposefulness. Dismissing the past, guidance people must decide what is now most important and significant about their work, what is of lesser importance, and what has no place among their activities. Until they make these decisions, they will continue to be the aimless "maids of all work" in the schools.

Training

Lack of focus is, of course, a direct outgrowth of the training most guidance workers receive. Unfortunately the problem is circular in nature, for lack of focus has also dictated the development of training programs throughout the years. Training programs actually came into being before anyone knew what they should include. Small wonder then that the early trainers had little or no focus to their programs except that demanded by their students or dictated by the special competencies and interests of the trainers themselves. These improvisations and penchants then became hallowed by tradition. The same lack of consistent focus has persisted throughout the history of guidance training programs and has resulted in workers' going out to their jobs unable to determine the relative importance of their varied activities.

Through the years, some training programs have emphasized measurement; others, vocations and occupational information; still others, administration; a few, modern counseling; but many more have presented a hodgepodge of all these areas, with little indication of the relative importance of each.[2] Even where there has been some definite emphasis within the training program, few guidance workers have developed the confidence and the

[2] A brief survey of the contents of any collection of introductory guidance textbooks will illustrate this dilemma.

conviction to implement it in their school programs. Focus, where it has existed, has usually been too vague or too unworkable to serve a useful purpose in practice.

Essentially, most training programs need considerable revision before they can realistically be expected to prepare people for effective work in the schools. The first of the needed reforms will have to come in the area of focus. If the focus is to be upon the individual student—as it must be if guidance is to have any place in the schools today—then every phase of the training program should be directed toward making this focus operational. And every guidance worker should leave his training knowing that his activities, whatever their specific nature, should center holistically around the student.

Revision within training programs naturally requires revised thinking among counselor trainers, and it is precisely at this point that many attempted reforms bog down. Counselor trainers today are of two types: those who have been trained as clinical or counseling psychologists, and those who have been trained in the more traditional areas of guidance work. Both groups have a vested interest in the type of training afforded them. Moreover, many trainers have devoted considerable time and energy to research and related activities and cannot easily relinquish these interests in favor of a new approach. When one has devoted years to the investigation of occupational information, the realization that most of this study is virtually useless in application in the schools comes hard, if at all. Vested interests and emotional commitment to certain specific kinds of courses and activities are perhaps the greatest stumbling blocks to the improvement of training programs.

State certification requirements are often blamed by counselor trainers for the retention of outmoded courses and the repetitiousness of much of the work in guidance. Certification requirements, however, are nothing but an institutionalized expression of the vested interests and emotional commitments of groups of counselors and counselor trainers and, as such, cannot be used to rationalize the inadequacies of training. Certification requirements can and will be altered if counselors really want to change them, but such changes will not come until guidance workers know where they are going and what they want.

Myths and actualities have definite implications for the directions in which training programs should go in the next few years. The most important reform concerns the development of courses specifically for guidance counselors. Most trainees take courses in measurement taught by measurement experts from their particular point of view. Probably such courses are necessary, but they are not sufficient. Guidance trainees need some work in measurement that will help them to determine the place of testing in their own programs, the ethical and humanitarian use of test results, and the interpretation of test results to students, parents, teachers, administrators, and members of the community.[3] Work along these lines is seldom if ever found in the usual measurement course, and most guidance workers acknowledge their lack of security in these areas.

Similarly, many trainees take a considerable number of psychology courses taught by psychologists and emphasizing the particular interests of the instructor. Again such courses may be necessary, but they are not sufficient for the school guidance worker whose concentration will be upon the "normal" child in the school setting. Guidance workers need an understanding of human behavior that will enable them to help students to deal with their problems, but this understanding must also be applicable and unfettered by specific, theoretical orientations or schools of psychology. Certainly the school counselor needs to know something about abnormal psychology and neurotic behavior, but he also needs to develop perspective upon this information and a realistic idea of the kinds of behavior he can expect to meet in his school. Guidance trainees actually need a

---

[3] Test interpretation is one of the least discussed areas in guidance and one of the most troublesome. For a new approach to the problem, see Ruth Barry and Beverly Wolf, *Developmental School Counseling*, to be published by the Bureau of Publications, Teachers College, Columbia University.

psychology of the "normal" human being, and perhaps the greatest contribution trainers could make would be to develop course work which presents positive views of human behavior.

Finally, guidance trainees take a number of courses centering around such informational areas as occupations, educational planning, and records.[4] Most of these courses have traditionally been taught for the purpose of making the trainee an informational expert, and here the loss of focus is obvious. If the counselor's concentration is to be upon the student, then the training program cannot give primary emphasis to information. Guidance theorists and trainers have failed to think through the informational role of the counselor and to implement this role in the kind of training offered. Some type of informational courses may be necessary for school guidance workers, but the concentration of such courses should be upon means of motivating students, helping them to locate and evaluate information for themselves, and broadening their horizons with respect to educational and vocational opportunities. All too often the informational courses center around the minutiae of the DOT, the advantages of one filing system over another, and the specifics of particular occupational brochures. Motivating students and enlarging their perspectives are rarely, if ever, treated in informational courses, and yet these are the problems the beginning guidance worker meets head on when he starts work in a school.

Informational courses in their present form persist in many training programs because of the vested interests, emotional commitment, and fear of some guidance leaders. They seem to feel that the informational courses are all that distinguish the training of a guidance worker from that of a psychologist or an educator and they fear that, without these courses, the

[4] Some training programs offer a semester course in the cumulative record. Perhaps the most needed change in focus in training is for trainers to regard their students as literate adults whose common sense and intelligence will enable them to cope with records—and even with the DOT—without this kind of puerile course work. If trainees actually need this kind of work, then, in the opinion of the authors, these trainees do not belong in counseling.

field itself would lose its identity. But if the sole unique competence of a guidance worker consists of the ability to use the DOT and an adeptness at filing occupational brochures, then perhaps guidance should be allowed to disappear. In making information paramount among guidance activities, trainers have fostered the growth of this fear and have contributed to the lack of development of training programs that are distinctly modern counseling in nature.

Guidance could be a distinct, well-defined field if the leaders, trainers, and theoreticians would adapt and synthesize the materials from other subject-matter areas into course work that is meaningful to and suitable for the school guidance worker. Such course work must of necessity represent a synthesis of information and research from other fields as well as from guidance itself. Trainees may well take measurement courses, but they should also take work in the use of testing techniques as they relate particularly to the counseling area. The entire measurement concept should be subordinated to the primary focus of guidance upon the individual student. Similarly, trainees should have some of the traditional courses in psychology taught by psychologists, but they should then be helped to synthesize these materials in terms of their particular work and the kinds of individuals with whom they will be working. Such a synthesizing experience should eliminate the tendencies of some guidance workers to regard themselves as psychologists with strong loyalties to some particular theoretical orientation and of others to regard their work as relatively nonpsychological and primarily advisory in nature. Synthesis of materials into a body of knowledge suitable for guidance workers will, moreover, define the field far more effectively than all the mythopoeic philosophical pronouncements of the past fifty years.

Synthesis and the establishment of courses distinctly designed for the school guidance worker are long overdue. For years guidance courses have been criticized as superficial, repetitious, ill-conceived, badly organized, and nonsequential. And, indeed, in many instances they are—for the trainee is taught to administer before he knows what it is he is to administer, to test before he knows why he is testing, or to advise about occupations before concepts of vocational development have even begun to come into being. Even more serious, however, has been the failure of trainers to incorporate into training courses some of the insights from sociology, anthropology, economics, and education that might aid trainees in their work in the schools. Even in psychology, trainers have limited their offerings to the abnormal aspects of human behavior and have tended to underplay the significant materials in developmental, educational, and experimental psychology and child study. If school counseling is to become a true academic field with a well-defined subject matter of its own, then synthesis of materials from all pertinent fields is a necessity, and only when this has been achieved will guidance people be able to claim with justification that their training enables them to offer something uniquely different from that provided by other forms of training.

Currently, some of the Institutes established under the National Defense Education Act are offering training that is beginning to approach a synthesis of materials suitable for school counseling trainees. In some of the Institutes where a modern counseling practicum occupies a central position in the program, trainees are acquiring a focus upon the high school student as an individual and are learning to see the other areas of guidance activity in perspective and as subsidiary to the counseling core. The progress toward synthesis made in some of the Institute programs may or may not have affected the regular programs of the universities in which they are located, but it is to be hoped that they will, for, in some respects and in some Institutes, the work represents the greatest advance in the history of guidance training.

Values

No discussion of the counselor can omit consideration of his values and the role they play in his work with students. Recognition of values and their importance is a recent development within the guidance and counseling field and, to date, has received attention chiefly from those workers with a counseling orientation. Vocational guidance specialists have seemingly remained less concerned about the effect of their values and of value conflicts upon students.

School counselors by and large are recruited from the ranks of teachers who generally are staunch upholders of middle-class values. Hence school guidance workers can usually be expected to support the values extolling work and the worth of education and encouraging long-range planning and postponed satisfactions. In this, present-day guidance people are simply perpetuating what have come to be called the traditional school values. Only recently have educators begun to realize that not all students—or adults—always subscribe to the same value system as that promulgated by the schools.

Educators support not only the values closely enmeshed with the school system but also those which they as individuals have learned in the course of their lifetimes. This stand means that students are expected to live up to the idiosyncratic values of their teachers and administrators as well as the traditional school values. When a student's values are in accord with those of the school and his teachers, he experiences little difficulty; when they are not, the student is frequently unable to make himself understood or to achieve even a partial adjustment within the school community.

School guidance people have for too long been unaware of the importance of values and value differences in their work with students. Recognition of the effects of values would have prevented the development of the advisory approach to guidance work, for advice cannot avoid being tainted by the values of the adviser and may, therefore, be completely at odds with the values of the advisee and the people significant to him. With the development of the counseling approach to guidance work, value conflicts have been recognized as disruptive, and attempts to eliminate them have made progress. As yet, however, the influence of values in the vocational area is largely unrecognized and vocational guidance practitioners have made few attempts to lessen their influence.

The lack of attention to values is another missing element in much of the guidance and counseling training of the past half century. Training has dealt with many of the superficial aspects of guidance and seldom ventured into the subtler, less tangible area of school and counselor values. When a guidance person advises a student to become a professional man, he is not merely offering advice, he is expressing his own values regarding the professions and urging on the student a long-term plan of education and establishment within the particular professional area. While there is nothing wrong with the values expressed by the adviser, they may not be right for the student receiving the advice. (In their work with students, school guidance people should be constantly aware of their own values and those of the school, so that they can be alert to the possible conflicts and ready to help those students caught in value conflicts. In most training programs there is little to prepare the guidance worker for this kind of difficulty. Trainees need considerable practice in recognizing their own values and those of others and in fostering an understanding of value differences and the rights of individuals to differing values.)

(The guidance worker who attempts to be a counselor to his students often encounters difficulties in recognizing his own personal value system, which may partially explain why there are so few counselors and so many advisers. Most counselors who have been teachers have to learn a new set of values when they become counselors. They have to give added recognition to the worth of each individual and be willing to accept each individual as unique. This is an easy value to acknowledge, but an inordinately difficult one to make operational. Counselors have to learn to value listening instead of talking; gradual resolving of problems instead of quick, verbal solving; and allowing the student to work things out for himself instead of telling him what to do. The values inherent in teaching are diametrically opposed to those of counseling, and the teachers who become counselors need considerable help in coping with these differences.

Traditional vocational guidance has operated on the assumption that everyone's values are the same, that everyone is ambitious and eager to get ahead, that everyone considers work of equal importance, and that all students share the feelings and desires of their vocational adviser. For this reason among many others, students have often found the vocational advice offered them completely unacceptable. This lack of awareness of the importance of values in working with individuals has long been a major stumbling block to the success of vocational guidance. Because vocational specialists have tended to adopt the concept that the career is the all-important factor, they have overlooked the fact that, for the individual, he and his values are all-important and the vocation is secondary except as it enhances, supports, and conforms to this value system. The history and failures of vocational guidance could be interpreted as a study of misunderstood and misplaced values.

Essentially counselors who want to deal successfully with the myths and actualities of the vocational area need a thorough understanding of the problems inherent in differing values. Without such an understanding they cannot analyze for themselves the values they are exemplifying in their actions, their relationships with students, and their program as a whole. Moreover, counselors need to interest themselves in values if they are truly to operate as counselors with their students. And finally, counselors have to understand their own values and those of the society in which they live if they are to become the kinds of people who can carry on an educational program suited to the second half of the twentieth century.

Person

Focus in his work, thorough professional training, and an understanding of values and value conflicts are, of course, necessary qualities for the counselor who is to conduct a program that is untraditional and up-to-date. Some beginners in guidance come to the work with some of these attributes fairly well developed, while others can in the course of their training—if it is truly training for modern counseling—acquire these essentials. But there are other counselor attributes that do not lend themselves to development through training, although they are equally important in the success or failure of the counselor on the job.

In most lists of the desirable characteristics of counselors, intelligence ranks low and yet, in the present state of guidance training, intelligence would seem to be a *sine qua non* for the effective counselor. If one defines intelligence as the ability to see relationships, to combine isolated bits of information into a coherent totality, then the importance of intelligence for the counselor is obvious. A counselor must be able to build in his mind a picture of each student with whom he works from the bits and pieces of information given him by the student, his teachers, his parents, and his records, and be able to operate from a constantly developing hypothesis. In this process, intelligence is an absolute requisite. Moreover, if the counselor is to take advantage of the training offered him at the moment he must be able to synthesize the materials presented, to draw his own conclusions, and to develop the practical applications for himself. Intelligence is a prime factor in enabling the trainee to utilize his training effectively.[5]

It seems strange that intelligence has for so long been relatively ignored as an important quality of future counselors. In part, this attitude seems to derive from the myth that the in-

[5] Any list of counselor qualities is of course purely hypothetical. We do not actually know what makes a good counselor. Our list is based upon our experience with trainees in class and practicum and the qualities we have observed in them which seem to enable them to operate effectively in their schools. Intelligence is one such quality, but it is intelligence as we have defined it, not as defined by scores on some of the intelligence tests. In other words, a high Miller Analogies score is not necessarily an indication of a good counselor, nor is a low one per se indicative of total ineptness in counseling.

telligent person cannot get along well with other people. In the light of increasing knowledge about giftedness, the illogicality of this assumption is immediately apparent. This attitude may also stem from the fact that intelligent trainees are not necessarily comfortable for trainers to have in class. Such trainees ask embarrassing questions, criticize programmatic arrangements, make suggestions for improvement, and tend to "rock the boat." Like educators in general, guidance trainers have tended to view such trainees as difficult to get along with and not good potential counselor material.

Intelligence, important as it is to the counselor, is not enough. To become a good counselor, a trainee has to have feeling for himself, for others, and for humanity as a whole. This quality has been summed up in many ways—empathy, understanding, approachability, good human relationships, identification, sympathy, and so on—but in essence it seems to consist of the ability to feel oneself and to accept those feelings, and to feel with others and accept their feelings without judgment. Some trainees have their own feelings so well masked that very little warmth, friendliness, or interest appears in their work with students. Intelligence without its emotional accompaniment, empathic acceptance, makes a counselor sterile and ineffective.

The feeling component necessitates considerable self-understanding on the part of the trainee. Some of his feelings are, of course, inappropriate if they are expressed in the course of his work. The trainee has to understand himself well enough to be able to master his irritations, frustrations, and worries and hold them in abeyance as he works with students. Perhaps the really successful counselor is able not only to understand himself but also to forget himself in his work with others.

In addition to intelligence, feeling, and self-understanding, counseling trainees need a certain amount of personal security. If he is to set up and develop a worth-while program in his school, a counselor needs confidence in himself and in his ability. Good training can provide him with some of this security, but in addition to professional competence, much of it seems to stem from his own inner conviction of personal worth and effectiveness. Counselor rewards and satisfactions come so indirectly and often so long after the fact, that the counselor needs this security to help him through the more difficult times in his work.

Perhaps security is most necessary for counselors in supplying them with the courage to do what they think is right for their students, their schools, and their communities. It takes courage to change a program, to curtail a testing program, to explain to a PTA why a child should not be forced to make an early vocational decision, and to sell a board of education on the concept of counseling as the core of a guidance program. Even the actual counseling process requires courage from the counselor, for all too often his entire background makes him fear the expression of feeling and his role as a counselor requires him to face and accept the emotions of his counselees, regardless of his own fears. Finally, a counselor needs the courage to say no, to reject some of the tasks which teachers and administrators want to foist off on him, and to do so in a manner that does not alienate either group. Courage without defensiveness, together with personal security, will enable the counselor to destroy the myths of vocational guidance and to develop a program in accord with the actualities of today.

Finally, a counselor needs flexibility. Not even the most forward-looking training program nor the most ardent crystal ball gazer can prepare for the future or predict it completely. Counselors need to be flexible in order to keep pace with the changes that will be the inevitable pattern of life in the next fifty years. But such flexibility must be based upon thoughtful understanding of the changes taking place and of their implications for the school and for counseling programs. Too often in the past, guidance workers were overly influenced by every fad and new idea that anyone cared to propound. Because of this tendency, guidance workers have been called wishy-washy and accused of not knowing where they stand. Flexibility represents a nice middle ground between overreceptivity to outside influences and the stubborn traditionalism that does not admit the existence of a new idea or a new need. Actually, flexibility grows out of focus and training in conjunction with the counselor's intelligence, feeling, self-understanding, security, and courage.

Perhaps most important of all, a counselor needs to be and to know that he is human, with all the virtues and faults that that word connotes. In many instances the lists of counselor attributes read like descriptions of medieval saints. It is unlikely that saintliness is a desirable attribute for the adult who is to work with twentieth-century adolescents. Rather counselors need the experience, tolerance, and humility that develop from learning to know and accept their own humanness and that of others.

Conclusion

The counselor who combines in his personal qualities and his focus and training some of the attributes discussed above will be able to deal knowingly and constructively with many of the problems discussed in this book. Such a counselor can tackle with courage the myths of traditional vocational guidance. Understanding the myths, he can discard them and build in their place a counseling program based upon thorough knowledge of adolescents and their problems today. He can incorporate in his program the actualities of today and the predictions for the future in such a way that he helps students learn to live with the anxiety and the challenge of constant change. This kind of counselor will view each of his students as a complete personality which cannot be subdivided into parts, phases, or aspects; and he will devise a program that recognizes this holism. In so doing, he will develop a program that really works for his school and community and that honestly meets the needs of his students as they attempt to find for themselves their places in the modern world. Such counselors—for there will be many of them—will eventually place the final period on the epitaph of traditional vocational guidance.

A Note on Readings

The literature of vocational guidance is voluminous but, as is so often true, quantity is no guarantee of quality. Most of the publications are traditional, repetitious, and lacking in originality. Most of them also fail to deal with some of the fundamental problems that guidance workers encounter in their schools. Many attempt to be too inclusive, to deal with vocational problems on all levels and in all settings when such an approach is patently impossible in terms of the persons involved.

The reader who wishes to pursue the consideration of vocational guidance further will find references to the important books in the field in the footnotes or text of this book. He should certainly read the works of Anne Roe and Donald Super for modern views of the field, and probably Frank Parsons' book for an idea of where it all began and how little actual progress has been made. For a statement of the traditional approach to vocational guidance and the recommended school program, almost any textbook in the area will serve. For current points of view toward the area, the reader may follow the articles in the *Personnel and Guidance Journal* and the *Vocational Guidance Quarterly*.

Caution is desirable in approaching the vocational guidance literature. The mere quantity of materials tends to convince some readers of the "rightness" of the points of view and ideas presented. In this particular field, however, readers should approach the literature forewarned and armed with both skepticism and powers of critical analysis. A thoughtful examination of the literature should enable readers to draw their own conclusions about the myths, actualities, and implications of traditional vocational guidance.

INDEX

INDEX